Enjoy sharing the walk
through these pages!

Christine Roche

Jan-2006.

FRONT COVER PHOTO: Chris Barnes, Christine Roche and Anne Ling on Dunnet Head, most northerly point of mainland Britain.

Printed in Victoria, BC, Canada

Note for Librarians: a cataloguing record for this book that includes Dewey Decimal Classification and US Library of Congress numbers is available from the Library and Archives of Canada. The complete cataloguing record can be obtained from their online database at:
www.collectionscanada.ca/amicus/index-e.html
ISBN 1-4120-2635-0

TRAFFORD

This book was published *on-demand* in cooperation with Trafford Publishing. On-demand publishing is a unique process and service of making a book available for retail sale to the public taking advantage of on-demand manufacturing and Internet marketing. On-demand publishing includes promotions, retail sales, manufacturing, order fulfilment, accounting and collecting royalties on behalf of the author.

Offices in Canada, USA, UK, Ireland, and Spain
***book sales for North America and international*:**
Trafford Publishing, 6E–2333 Government St.
Victoria, BC V8T 4P4 CANADA
phone 250 383 6864   toll-free 1 888 232 4444
fax 250 383 6804   email to orders@trafford.com
***book sales in Europe*:**
Trafford Publishing (UK) Ltd., Enterprise House, Wistaston Road Business Centre
Crewe, Cheshire CW2 7RP UNITED KINGDOM
phone 01270 251 396   local rate 0845 230 9601
facsimile 01270 254 983   orders.uk@trafford.com
***order online at*:**
www.trafford.com/robots/040463.html

10 9 8 7 6 5 4 3 2

FOLLOW THE SPRING NORTH

- LAND'S END TO
JOHN O'GROATS

*For all those who are mentioned in these
pages, and all who added to the wonderful experience of the walk, and all who
thought of me while I was away.*

CHRISTINE ROCHE

INTRODUCTION

"Live Your Dream!" The words in an advert in a free local paper caught my eye. That is what I must do, I thought. It has been at the back of my mind for ages. When did I first dream of walking from Land's End to John O'Groats? I started backpacking in 1979 - Offa's Dyke was the dream then, lived and walked that year, but it must have been a few years later, perhaps about 1990 or soon after, when I had thoughts of a LEJOG route, using the Wye Valley walk and the Lancashire coast as part of the route because I remember writing a poem, which I can't remember now, about it in the early 1990s. It is not just a walk, walking each day, or even a short holiday, soon over, but it is a way of life, lived for about three months.

It is pleasant to dream of what you would like to do. You can dream for years. You can stand on a hill and see into the distance and think, "Wouldn't it be marvellous to walk from down there right up the country past here and on northward!" From dream to practicalities, you know that something like that takes time, time to walk and even more time for preparations. Time like that has to wait for retirement. In the meantime you can collect some maps and have ideas about a possible route. First ideas change: would I enjoy the Lancashire coast with all that built up area to walk through? Road walking can cause blisters. Although I'd walked the Pennine Way many years ago I liked the route, love the Pennines and would be happy to include it. The Wye Valley would fit in with Offa's Dyke, which I had already walked, so how about walking the Wye Valley in 2002 then in 2003 using the Cotswold Way, Heart of England Way and Staffordshire Way on my LEJOG route instead?

The route I chose to walk eventually was determined partly by offers from friends and family to take food parcels, or the position of camp sites or hostels, but mostly by what I knew, or expected, to be a scenic route, avoiding roads as much as possible. I included areas I had not visited before and areas in which I had previously enjoyed walking. I wanted variety so, while I could have walked much further along the South West Coast Path, Bodmin Moor made a change from coastal scenery. Over the whole route I had great variety: coast (from cliffs and rocks to sand and dunes), riverside, moorland, field paths, bridleways, farm tracks, quiet lanes with hedgerows full of flowers and birds, hills, mountains, woodland, stony tracks or the softness of grassy ones, peat bogs, villages with friendly shops, cities with cathedrals, ancient ways and old bridges or modern bridges such as Kessock or Cromarty. My collection of maps increased. I started more serious and detailed planning. The planning and preparations took about a year.

I had carried a week's food before, so first thoughts were that a series of 12 food parcels would supply me for the whole walk, although smaller parcels were sometimes more convenient or if recipients lived less than 7 days apart. Later I sent extra food parcels with fewer days' supply to save weight. Having had a dehydrator for a few years helped; I had a stock of dehydrated meat, vegetables, fruit, cooked long grain rice, even some baked beans, and more foods were dehydrated, labelled and packed. These parcels would go to friends and family, to campsites or hostels. I did not send them to Post Offices in case I arrived after they had closed or on a Saturday afternoon, when I should have to wait until Monday morning to collect them.

Much time was spent browsing over maps, marking them with arrows to show my intended routes. Sometimes maps were cut, if only a corner were required, or much of the map included sea, or the route was on half the map only - why carry the weight, or why post home the extra weight? In some cases sections of map were photocopied when just part of a map was required, and the backs of these photocopies could also be written on as diary pages. From a few maps I also trimmed the margins. Envelopes, large plastic ones, were address labelled and some of them stamped, after being weighed at the Post Office with a couple of maps inside, and included in each parcel ready to send maps home when I had walked off them. You can certainly dream looking at maps. You also plan possible overnights - is there a campsite or likely farm or wild pitch, or family or friend or member of the Backpackers Club or, failing these, a hostel? I worked out these possibilities allowing about 15 miles per day, a comfortable distance to walk, I find.

"Follow the Spring North" had also been part of my plan. Spring is one of my favourite seasons for walking because new life can be seen all around, in fresh opening greenery and spring flowers, and heard in birdsong as you walk or as you lie in your tent. New birds arrive from overseas. Primroses and daffodils can be seen in southwest England in March, further north in April, and flowering in Scotland in May. It was a continual pleasure to keep seeing "The first wood anemone...." or other first flower of the spring as I moved northward. The weather in spring is not normally too hot for walking, although I have known many weeks in Scotland in May with summer heat, but snow is possible too. However, the one day's snow that I walked through was in the centre of England. To arrive in Scotland in the summer would mean all the midges coming to welcome you. (I carried a small part-used bottle of midge repellent from Edinburgh but did not need it). In spring the quality of light is something special, not blazing down hard from above as in summer, but more usually a soft, clear brightness shining at an easy angle to emphasise the shape of hills, farm buildings or trees or whatever is in that particular landscape. The hours of daylight are increasing.

People asked if I was doing it for charity. I thought I might as well since I was walking all that way, so sponsor forms were prepared and time spent collecting signatures and cash, for three charities actually: Hearing Dogs for Deaf People, Christian Aid for clean water supplies for Mali (near the Sahara) where something in the water causes blindness, and St Mary's Church, Sandbach for disabled access. All these things took time, and time went quickly.

Clothing was planned, with items that were quick drying and lightweight. Boots were well broken in. The tent and other items of equipment were checked - was a stitch in time needed? Small containers were filled with toothpaste and environmentally friendly cleanser, which can be used for washing self, clothes, hair, or pans, based on coconut oil. The only new items bought for the walk were a waterproof mobile phone case and waterproof camera case; I didn't want either of these to stop working due to getting wet. Other items were well tried and tested. Most importantly, I had to remember at least two sheets of paper in each parcel for the diary writing, and a pen of course, and a spare pen. These would be carried in the mapcase to keep them handy, and the paper dry and flat. I had to work out how much cash I'd be likely to need and take it mostly in £5 notes and pound coins because more often than not, I should be buying small quantities of food in village shops and should not want to offer £10 or more to be changed. I found that I spent about £12.50 per week on such things as rolls and cheese for lunches, fruit and tomatoes, fresh milk, chocolate and cakes for extra calories and, when I got the chance, a pot of tea and cake worked wonders! Pitch fees for camping were the unknown quantity; I could be charged a lot for very little, or a reasonable charge for excellent facilities, or "Oh, nothing if you're doing it for charity!" Those wonderful wild pitches with outstanding views cost nothing!

The writing of a diary is something I have done for several years on walks of longer than a weekend. Memorable though a walk is at the time, the details can soon be forgotten, but if a diary is written each night, or next morning, while the experiences and sights and sounds of the day are fresh in your mind they will be there for you to read in the future and recall those happy days. That is what this diary was to be - something to read and re-live, something to read again in old age, an account of those three special months, a sort of letter written to myself. Then first Anne-Marie Edwards (author of some excellent books of walks in Hampshire, Dorset and Somerset) then Anita Burden (a friend from Sandbach) suggested that it should be made into a book. This book is the result. The actual pages typed out from my original pages of small writing are now in a folder with miscellaneous items stuck in. These include: a Post Office receipt for a food parcel I sent off, a few photos, some till receipts detailing food I bought on my travels, actual labels from food, such as Wensleydale cheese, Walkers Gingerbread Cake, and my favourite Co-op Fairtrade Dark Chocolate, train tickets, postcards (one sent by my aunt in 1979 from John O'Groats), one or two letters of encouragement or congratulation, and some leaflets from such places as Forsinard Nature Reserve, John O'Groats Camp Site and Duncansby Head.

Finally, all the food parcels were out of the way, delivered or posted to the people who were looking after them for me; a train ticket was booked for Penzance and a night booked at a hostel there. For the previous few months the welcome message on my mobile phone had been, and still was "LIVE YOUR DREAM!" and shortly I was going to live it!

MAPS FOR LEJOG

OS Mapping Index 2002 - for choosing the maps required.
Total Maps used: Landrangers **36,**
Explorer/Outdoor Leisure **6.**
The numbers on the maps are correct but the names may not correspond with those printed on the map, some being those of places on the route.

Land's End to Cheltenham:

Landranger	203	Land's End
	200	Newquay
	201	Bodmin Moor
Explorer	112	Launceston
	113	Okehampton
	127	South Molton
Landranger	181	Dulverton
	193	Taunton
	182	Glastonbury
	183	Yeovil
	172	Bristol, Bath
	162	Gloucester
	163	Cheltenham

Cheltenham to Macclesfield

	150	Worcester & The Malverns
	151	Stratford on Avon
	139	Birmingham
	128	Derby
	127	Stafford
	118	Stoke on Trent

Macclesfield to Edinburgh

Outdoor Leisure	24	White Peak
	109	Manchester
Outdoor Leisure	21	South Pennines
	103	Burnley
	98	Wensleydale & Upper Wharfedale
	91	Appleby
	86	Haltwhistle
	80	Cheviots
	74	Kelso
	67	Duns, Dunbar

| 66 | Edinburgh |

Edinburgh to John O'Groats

Explorer	350	Edinburgh, South Queensferry
	58	Lomond Hills
	52	Perth
	43	Blair Atholl
	35	Glen Feshie, Kincraig
	26	Inverness
	21	Alness, Bonar Bridge
	16	Lairg
	17	Helmsdale
	10	Melvich
	12	Thurso & Wick

(John O'Groats, ferry to Burwick, South Ronaldsay) Orkney

| 7 | Orkney, Mainland |

DIARY OF LAND'S END TO
JOHN O'GROATS WALK

Wednesday 5th March 2003.
Land's End to Pendeen Watch:

Yesterday seemed like a dream. After the months of preparation and plans, it seemed unreal - Anita picking me up at 2.30pm, then David and Pauline joining us on Crewe Station to see me off from platform one. Anita took a photo of me in the train doorway, then we were waving, the train was moving and I was on the way. I later looked out at misty Cotswolds and wondered what they'd be like when I got that far on the walk.....then, hours later, I eventually arrived at Penzance a few minutes early. Anne and Chris, who were to accompany me for the first three days, were there to meet me for the 20-minute walk to the Blue Dolphin backpackers' hostel in Alexandra Road. After a celebration with the wine and chocolates that I'd brought, we went to our room where we were joined by Bryan and Ron (also Backpackers Club members), after their first day's walking. They were walking from Land's End to John O'Groats by a different route, having started the previous day. I managed to sleep when the loud snores subsided!

We woke to find it raining, got up and had breakfast. There wasn't much to pack before getting the 9.25am bus to Land's End (£3). The rain even dripped through the roof of the bus shelter while we were waiting. I think the bus arrived at Land's End about 10 o'clock. I found where to get a form for the LEJOG Club, to be signed at places on the way, where I camp overnight or at a hostel, then Chris took a photo of me near the signpost. I think the signpost stated "874 miles" but that must be the distance by road. I had estimated that my route would be about 1,200 miles. It had almost stopped raining. Now we were actually on the Coast Path, passing the First and Last House, onward on the first stage of the walk with the Isles of Scilly faint on the horizon, which was becoming lighter as we walked on. The rain stopped; the band of blue increased as we continued over easy paths or rocky sections. At Aire Point we stopped for lunch, sitting in the sun, delighting in the blue of sea and sky, then we continued in T-shirts, waterproofs no longer needed.

There were celandines and violets and we'd seen primroses earlier; the flowers and the weather made it seem like the first day of spring. At first the waves seemed to move beachwards in slow motion - later they crashed against rocks, sending spray high in the air.

We passed the old tin mine buildings, walked through Bottalack first, all in sunshine. At Portheras Cove a stream runs down a deep valley to the sea, after Pendeen Watch lighthouse. We crossed on stepping-stones then collected our water supply for the night, being uncertain if we'd find more before we pitched. It was hard work carrying water as well as heavy packs up the steep slope to the cliff tops, then easier when we reached the top, although it was some way along a muddy path before Chris, ahead, found a level grassy pitch. Much of the area was covered in gorse and brambles where it was not possible to pitch. We just managed to get the tents up in daylight, about 6.45pm, then cooked our meals and looked out at the starry sky. What a lovely first day of this long walk! Now to sleep, with the sound of the sea below. (12½ - 13 miles).

Thursday 6th March
- Portheras Cove to St Ives:

That was certainly a beautiful pitch now we could see it in the light of a spring-like morning. The sun shone into the tents as we had our breakfast and packed, eager to be on our way. First we came to some old mine buildings then, after ½ mile of cliff top walking we came to a very boggy stretch of path and couldn't get round it (Anne said she saw a shoe in it!) so we diverted to an overgrown, concessionary path and eventually had to cross a field or two to reach the lane then we walked about three miles along the quiet road before returning to the coast path. The weather remained sunny and spring-like so we were walking in T-shirts again. At Zennor we went in the pub (was it the Tinners?) where, in spite of the sign in the window saying so, they were not serving tea, so Anne and I had water for refreshment; we preferred tea or water at this time of day.

We continued by level field paths on a straight, grassy way with stone "cattle grid" stiles, very effortless to cross, like I'd seen on the Isles of Scilly in 2001. When a small group of walkers passed us I asked what the path was, whether it was an old way, and was told that it was a "Coffin Way." We were also told that a ruined chapel we'd just seen used to be the "Ranters," who danced about causing the floor to give way. What a shock for them! This easy path continued until we came to a farm where we had to pick our way through deep, wet mud to the stile, then the next farm was worse. These farms were near Clodgy Point, so we called it *clodgy* mud or muck. After this there were clean, green fields taking us to the outskirts of St Ives. We talked to two small grey ponies over a gate at the lane, and then descended into St Ives. We were going to camp in the garden of some friends of theirs so Chris eventually walked on to find the house, after a fair distance along roads. We were very glad to arrive, have cups of tea and showers, pitch the tents then have a lovely meal. We returned, contentedly tired, to our tents on the lawn.....I remember seeing thrift growing on the cliffs, but it could have been yesterday.

Friday 7ᵗʰ March 2003
- St Ives to Portreath:

We woke to birdsong from the surrounding trees and rain pattering on the tents. We made breakfast in our tents but Norma came out with mugs of tea and asked us in for more tea and toast. We were talking so didn't set out until 10 o'clock, which didn't matter as it was raining. However, the rain had stopped by the time we had walked up the lane. Phil and Norma had suggested using part of St Michael's Way to avoid walking through St Ives to Hayle. We had trouble finding the stile in the caravan site with no waymarks to guide us, but after a couple more fields the continuation across a lane was a pleasant wooded path past a cottage and up to a road, after which there was no signpost for a path on the other side so we climbed a gate and a bank to reach a stile past a house, Rock Bowl Chapel, and field paths to the road to Hayle. We saw a sign "Teas" at Griggs Quay Tearooms and couldn't resist going in for a pot of Earl Grey and a bite to eat at a table in the large window overlooking the estuary. Besides the many gulls out there we saw a curlew, an oystercatcher and a redshank.

With renewed energy we walked through Hayle, buying some fruit and eggs at a shop on the way, then we turned the corner towards the beach and the path over the sand dunes. We soon left this path to walk on the firm sand with the wind right behind us. Anne was seen sailing along ahead to our right and I asked Chris to take a photo of me on my camera (he actually took two, the noise of the wind preventing him from hearing the film move on) as we all went at a fair pace for about three miles along the beach with very little effort. This was really exhilarating, striding over the sand with the sea to our left and a lighthouse on a rock ahead. Near the headland, Godrevy Point, we left the beach on a track and stopped for a snack in the shelter of some gorse bushes. We reckoned that the wind had pushed us along the beach at 5m.p.h!

Due to the strong wind, we omitted Godrevy Point and walked a stretch of quiet road before joining the Coast Path again at Hell's Mouth, but we were soon blown about so Anne asked if we could return to the road. When the Coast Path came alongside again we rejoined it and appreciated the shelter of the gorse bushes until the force of the wind hit us on the open cliff tops, especially where it funnelled up a valley. We had forded the little stream being afraid of being blown off the plank footbridge! There was one point where I froze, leaning on my poles, being sure that if I lifted one leg I'd be blown off the other leg and into the barbed wire fence. Finally, on the last section of cliff before Portreath we heard the wind roaring in our ears, felt it strengthening and threw ourselves to the ground, keeping down until the worst had passed. Phew! At least we were not blown where we didn't want to go and the wind was blowing landwards not seawards! It was now 6 o'clock and we were only 10-15 minutes walk from Portreath, down a sheltered valley path. We went into the Waterside Inn for hot coffee while waiting for Phil and Norma to pick us up for a further night in their garden. Two pub customers gave donations of £5 and £2 for my sponsored walk and we looked out of the window at the waves crashing against the breakwater in the dusk, then emerged into the darkness to be taken back for welcome mugs of tea, bath/shower and another good meal in pleasant company, discussing books we'd read, until, yawning, we went out to the tents in the sheltered garden for another good night's sleep.

Saturday 8th March
- Portreath to Perranporth, Perran Beach:

Phil and Norma, with Anne and Chris aboard, kindly returned me to Portreath for the next section of Cornish coastal walking. I realised that I'd forgotten to take a photo of the tents in their garden

- too late now. I ascended to a less windy cliff top, enjoying walking above the breaking waves on a sea that was turquoise near the cliffs and grey in the distance with a cloudy horizon and sky. It had been lovely sharing the first three days with Anne and Chris but I was quite happy walking on my own.

At Porthtowan I tried phoning Dad from a phone box but there was no reply so I phoned Anita. A few miles further on at St Agnes at about 1.50pm I got through to Dad to tell him about the walk. Round St Agnes Head had been very windy and just round the point I'd been blown off my feet, sideways onto the heather slope above the path. Further on, now heading eastward, it was easier with the wind not as strong and behind me. A sheltered seat made a good lunch stop, but only a quick one, then I stopped when I saw a sheltered grassy hollow where I could sit comfortably and take off boots and socks to air my feet. I also wrote half of yesterday's diary, being too tired to write when we went back to our tents last night, then, refreshed and rested, I walked on towards Perranporth. I descended to the beach there via steps at the south end leading to some rocks then sand. A wide, fast flowing stream had stepping stones to cross it. Thank goodness the wind didn't blow me off into the water! I then made for a building near the top of the beach, which turned out to be "The Watering Hole" where I ordered a pot of tea and a doughnut. After this I collected water for the night and walked along beach, cliff, and dunes, then beach again as the tide went out, to the north end of Perran Beach, where Norma had said there was a wild pitch in the dunes and had pencilled an arrow to it on the map. I am safely installed in a sheltered hollow in the dunes, protected from wind and waves, which make music below me. I have walked about 14½ miles today.

Saturday 9th March
- Perranporth to Bedruthan Steps:
The crashing of waves on the beach below was the first sound I heard this morning, having slept well in my sandy hollow. I was off at 9.30 and up on to the windy cliffs. Besides several skylarks I saw a hawk, possibly a peregrine, sailing, then swooping low over the ground near Penhale Camp, before I came down to Holywell. Here I decided to take the path over to Treago and Crantock, and from Crantock the lane down to the footbridge over the Gannel. The tide was out! That did save some miles of walking round by road. I

walked across the sandy estuary to the footbridge on which a group of people stood, but they remained there and I had to squeeze past - they were mostly youngsters fishing. Nobody fell off.

There was quite a bit of road and pavement walking into Newquay, which was tiring. Lunch was on an exposed seat overlooking the sea, where a few surfers were not having much success. I was glad to move on and get through this built-up area. I actually found some toilets that were open (most in Newquay were locked) and I was able to get water from a tap in the disabled toilet. A few minutes later I realised that I'd put my glasses down on the basin so returned for them. Next a short beach walk and a short road walk took me to a Coast Path sign and the relief of grass again under my feet. Now, high on the cliffs once more, I could stride along between fences where the path had been moved inland due to "unstable cliffs." Rain gently pattered, then became more wetting so I stopped to put on waterproofs, then it stopped, of course. The wind increased so I used the path signed "Trevarrian" then went by road to Porth Mawgan, where there was not a lot to see, except rows of modern bungalows terracing the hillside. There was rain again. I began to think about a possible pitch - I could ask at a farm, or would there be water at Bedruthan Steps National Trust car park? The NT tearooms (open 11-4) were closed of course, also the toilets, but - welcome sight! - on the side of the building was a tap marked "Drinking Water." I drank what was left in my water bottle, filled it and half filled the waterbag. It then took some searching to find a pitch sheltered from the wind on the cliff tops, until I eventually found one beside a bank, breezy but out of the full force of the wind. I was ready for a mug of tea and a meal, which I enjoyed. Next I had a wash and did my washing, and then I wrote my diary until ready for sleep after a 15 mile day.

Monday 10th March
- Bedruthan Steps to wild beyond Wadebridge:

It was still breezy when I woke, and cloudy but dry. I could hear gulls calling and a lark singing, for a good start to the day. I had porridge, dehydrated baked beans (soaked overnight) and a mug of tea, packed then set off at five past nine down to Bedruthan Steps. I took a photo but there was no access to the beach, then continued upward followed by easy, level cliff tops. The 3½ miles to Porthethan took an hour and a half. A hot drinks sign tempted me to buy a mug of hot chocolate, also a bar of chocolate and an apple. After 15 minutes break at a picnic table there I headed up to the cliffs once more, stopping now and then to look in awe at the height of the spray as waves broke against the rocks and foam blew on to the cliffs. This area was rich in skylarks, some having little fear but walking quite close before taking off to rise for a short burst of song. I also heard a wren and an occasional raven. From Tregarnon I went up the lane to Constantine Bay, which had a useful shop where I bought bread - a round brown cob full of seeds and grains - and a tin of pilchards for lunch on the rocks at Harlyn Bay. (I took a photo of the bread and pilchards and apple on the polythene sheet at the base of the cliff). From here I followed the coast path to Trevone, then turned up the lane for Porthmissen and along the bridleway to Trethillick, then a path across a couple of fields brought me to the lane leading down Church Street in Padstow. The church clock struck three soon after I'd passed it then, at twenty past three, after taking a photo of the harbour, I started the Camel Trail when I eventually found the start; I had to ask where it was - I thought it would be clearly signed. Beside the track there were primroses, hart's tongue fern and blackthorn was flowering. Seats, placed where there was an open view of the Camel, gave encouragement to sit down and get out the binoculars. The most common bird was the oystercatcher, then the redshank, then the curlew. I think I saw two common sandpipers. There was also one cormorant. At last I had to press on for Wadebridge, for there was no water or camping possible before that.

I made my way up to the campsite shown on the map at Bodieve, but they wouldn't let me camp - they said they were closed (it did not say so on the big sign outside) and had no water on at the toilet block, and when I asked where they suggested they said St Kew, which was about 3 miles along the main road and I'd already walked 17 ½ miles, so I went on along the lane then down the track northward to a stream…water! Now I am comfortably pitched beside the track, having enjoyed plenty of tea and a meal, had a good wash of self and socks and written a postcard of Bedruthan Steps to Dad. I also phoned Tony Wilson, who wants me to update my whereabouts for his website/map. Apart from the unfriendly campsite it has been an enjoyable, varied and satisfying day of about 18 miles.

Tuesday 11th March 2003
- from near Wadebridge to Bodmin Moor, past Candra:

It was a peaceful night with not a sound of traffic before seven o'clock, although I was not far from the A39. This morning's birds were: thrush, robin, chaffinch, wren, pheasant, and wood pigeon - a change from the coastal birds. There was light drizzle this morning so I packed a damp tent then I got warm walking in Gore-Tex, so I used my umbrella while wearing the windshirt later on. Using the umbrella meant that I didn't need my hood up. Pleasant walking on lanes and bridleways brought me to Helland Bridge, the oldest mediaeval bridge on the Camel, other old ones having previously been destroyed in floods. I also stopped at the old Celtic cross at the crossroads soon after starting but there was no information to tell its age or why it was there. I now walked on another, more wooded, length of Camel Trail. The rain had stopped. There were more primroses here, celandines and common golden saxifrage. The miles passed quickly then I came to a stile on to the river bank just before Poley Bridge, the end of the trail, so I stopped at half past twelve for an early lunch, eaten as I sat leaning against a tree with boots and socks off. I had more of that delicious bread with pilchards, then Christmas cake; I'd eaten the banana earlier before it got too squashed.

At St Mabyn there was a friendly village shop/Post Office where I posted a postcard, put rubbish in the bin, then bought 2 apples, 2 eggs, a pint of milk and a double sachet of Ovaltine. At Blisland I could see no shop so it was just as well that I had bought those items before. I now headed for Bradford then Hawk's Tor Farm, which Phil and Norma had said was uninhabited so it would be all right to camp on the Tor behind it, but it was now inhabited so I had a look at the stone circle then returned to Bradford (I saw the ford next to the bridge) then went along a footpath to Delford Bridge, up the lane to the track leading to Irish Farm then I left the track for the path over the moor (part of Bodmin Moor), but I missed a right turn - an Explorer map would have been useful here - and came to the Candra farm track. At Candra I asked about camping and was told that I could go on the moor, with pure water from their "overflow" pipe just down the track. I carried water for about 20 minutes over the hill to where the wall turned a corner and gave shelter from the stiff breeze - but it was nothing like the previous days' winds! After a delicious meal of dehydrated coley, peas and

celery in parsley sauce with mash, then Cadbury's Chocolate dessert, I phoned Geoff Trevarthen about tomorrow, then Dad, Joyce,
Jim & Maggie (who were not in) and Anne Ling, before washing
self and clothes and I am now ready for sleep. Just a few buzzards
to add to the birdlife today. I am pitched near King Arthur's Hall, so
it says on the map, which I'll see tomorrow. I wonder what it is like.
Today was another good day.

Wednesday 12th March
- Bodmin Moor to Coad's Green:

What a lovely wild pitch with a view across Bodmin Moor and early
sunlight between passing clouds. It was now a cool east wind and
I set off at ten past nine in woolly hat and gloves. King Arthur's
Hall was only five minutes' walk away, a rectangular earthwork
with stones inside, parts of doorways, and rushes filling the centre. I took two photos, one from each of the nearest two corners,
then continued over the moor on easy short turf, then descended
to the stream, which was quite deep here, and looked for a place
to cross. I eventually found some large rocks, which gave a solid
crossing, then I had to squeeze between trees to reach the path
through the wood to the stile. A grassy track led from here round
the hillside then dropped from the old farm buildings, seen on the
photo, to a couple of wooden footbridges. White waymarks on
posts marked the route across moorland with the ridge of Brown
Willy (420 metres) ahead. Now I was ascending the ridge, warm in
the cold wind, occasionally sheltered by rocks, feeling at home in
this moorland area although I'd never been there before. I took a
photo between outcrops of rock and another at the summit, looking SSW towards the sea. I sat behind rocks just below the summit
cairn to have a bit of early lunch at 11.45, meaning to have the
rest later, but with concentrating on the route I didn't remember
to finish it until 3.25pm at Five Lanes near Altarnun. I had made
for the empty isolated farm at Leskernich, via a river crossing on
mossy stones, (the poles were useful to prevent slipping here), then
a barbed wire fence on a wall and a couple of gates to climb - they
had old, rusty padlocks on. From here I headed due east up the hill
to reach a stone circle; straight on from the circle was the bridleway
- on the map but not on the ground. I headed in the right direction,
then thought it best and quicker to make for the farm at Hendra (I
wonder if that is the same as the Welsh "Hendre") then ¾ mile be-

side the A30 to Trewint and Five Lanes. After this I seemed to make good time along the lanes and paths southward and I was pleased to find that there *was* a footbridge over the River Lynher, south of Knighton, although not marked as such on the map. I was making for Coad's Green, and phoned Geoff Trevarthen from Trebartha to say that I'd soon be there. I spent a very pleasant evening after a lovely meal with Geoff and Wendy at Coad's Green, and then slept indoors on my Z-Rest, having received and unpacked my first food parcel.

Thursday 13th March
- Coad's Green to Milford Farm, near Lifton:

Of course, we were talking for ages after breakfast, then we had coffee, so it was late when I left Wendy and Geoff on a sunny spring day. After we'd taken photos of each other I walked the eight miles to Launceston on sunny lanes and a footpath, with lambs in fields, primroses, celandines, daffodils, green fields and blue sky. After lunch in the sun on a wide grass verge I walked on into Launceston and visited Tesco, which the route passed, for lunch items and Yeo Valley yoghurt. The girl on the quick till was very friendly. Next I found, and took a photo of, the castle, bought some postcards (the cheapest on the whole walk, at 15p each!) then found my way out of town on the Two Castles Way. The Two Castles are Launceston and Okehampton. The crossing of the Tamar at Polden Bridge was a real landmark, the end of the Cornwall chapter!

Now in Devon, the way passed Welltown Farm on field paths then on lanes to Lifton Down and Lifton. On the lane from Lifton I asked a man leading a chestnut horse from a field if he had anywhere I could camp for the night, as it would soon be dusk. He said the land was all rented here but he thought that along the bridleway at Milford Farm (two miles from Lifton, and on my route anyway) would be all right. It was. I knocked at the backdoor and a man told me where to pitch and where the facilities were, having asked if he was allowed to permit camping. I said, "Yes, for up to 28 nights a year."

A rough grassy paddock gave a comfortable night; a toilet with hot and cold water was just across the track. I had been told to switch the immersion heater on in the ladies' toilet for the hot water, which was welcome. After a nice, warm wash I returned to the tent as a bright light shone on to it - the moon! A mug of tea and a meal were followed by phoning Tony Wilson to report on my progress and enquire after Bryan and Ron. He said they were having foot and hip trouble the day before, had had B&B at Launceston and were planning easier days.

The most common birds today and yesterday were buzzards. There were pheasants, blackbirds and a loud chirrup of sparrows in the hedges between Coad's Green and Launceston.

A good day of 16 miles.

Friday 14th March
- Milford Farm to Patchacott:

A still night and clear sky gave condensation on the flysheet but the sun soon dried most of it, also the T-shirt that I'd washed and hung from a fallen tree. I heard tawny owls last night. I didn't hurry with the packing so that the tent and washing would have more time to dry and because I should slow down a bit, do fewer miles, so as to get to Chenson camping barn on Sunday not Saturday night. I left at 9.35 and took a photo of the sign at the bottom of the track, then continued along sunny lanes, so sunny that I needed to remove the warm North Cape top, then at Broadwoodwidger I stopped to change the film in my camera. I could sit in a bus shelter to do this. I also wrote a postcard to Jan (next door) then posted the cards and film. I soon reached Roadford Lake, where I stopped for a pot of tea and carrot cake just before 12 o'clock (inside the building due to cool breeze over the picnic tables) but I had a lovely view over the lake. I also wrote this diary up to date while at the table, as it wasn't at all crowded.

However, a party of elderly and disabled people came in and were directed to the reserved table in front of mine. This provided entertainment: "Ida, do you want to sit next to Ken?"

"No, I don't want to sit next to Ken."

"Right, well you sit here then, next to Mollie."

Their meal came. Ida: "What is it?" Helper: "Chicken casserole." "I don't like chicken casserole." "You like chicken, Ida." "But I don't like chicken casserole." "Well, it's a set meal." "*You're* not having it." "No. I'm a vegetarian."

One of the catering staff: "We have a Cornish pasty - would you like a Cornish pasty, Ida?" "Yes, please, I'll have a Cornish pasty." It was duly brought and placed in front of her: Ida said it was too big!

I've only walked 4 miles this morning so I'd better get on, after buying some fudge (not too heavy to carry for a couple of days) for Jean. On I went in sun and breeze beside the lake until I came to the bird hide, so I stopped for a little while but there were not many birds about in the wind. I saw two great crested grebes and possibly a little grebe but it was too far away for me to be certain. Nothing came to the bird table or empty feeder of course, but a bluetit came to a nearby tree.

I continued round the lake to the picnic tables north of Headson Cross and stopped for my pilchard roll before going up to the lane where there were large clumps of primroses further on, then up to the footpath from Southweek wood, which made a nice change of scene and gave shelter from the east wind, to the ford and footbridge. In this wood there was a signpost where footpaths crossed, each of the four arms helpfully stating "FOOTPATH." I followed the path from Weeks Mill to Eworthy and paused in a wooden shed-type bus shelter to turn over the map, then continued past Bangors Farm and along the bridleway that passes Northcombe Stud. This bridleway is 1½ miles long, the latter part having deep wheel-ruts, some of them filled with water, so I was dodging between ruts and horse-trodden centre. Later, the hedge shelter on my right was no longer there so, with no protection from the cold east wind, I stopped to put on the North Cape top, stopping under a tree and having some chocolate while I was stopped, then when I reached the end of the bridleway I decided to put gloves on too.

Across the A3079 there was welcome hedge shelter. It was now late in the afternoon so at Patchacott I decided to ask at a farm for a sheltered spot to camp. Patchacott seemed to be all farms - no other houses. At the first farm there was nobody in; at the second there were aggressive sounds from a dog, but at the third first a friendly black and white collie, then friendly people at Bailey's Farm, the last of the group, on the right-hand side of the road. After consulting with each other about the suitability of various fields they thought the lawn would be most sheltered: "She said it was a small tent." Having shown me the water-tap and toilet and the lawn, they asked me in for a cup of tea. "That would be nice - I'll just pitch the tent and be there in a few minutes," I said. I quickly pitched and put things under cover then went in to sit at the kitchen table with them and enjoy a mug of tea, also a plate of vegetables, potatoes and mushrooms left from their meal, and have a chat with them before going back to the sheltered lawn to cook my own meal, which I have just enjoyed and have checked that I've done 13 miles on the map. I phoned Jim & Maggie to say where I am; they will pass the message on to Tony Wilson. I'm sitting in the light and warmth of a nightlight. The wind is roaring in the trees but the tent only moves slightly on this sheltered lawn behind the farmhouse - an ideal pitch for a windy night.

Saturday 15th March 2003
- Patchacott via Hatherleigh to Exbourne:

That was lovely, to sleep well, sheltered from the wind, then wake to a touch of frost on a sunny morning. I took a photo of the tent before I left. Phil and Jane Wonnacott are the people here, lovely friendly people too, so I mentioned the Backpackers' Farm Pitch Directory to them.

I walked by lane and field path to Northlew, where I bought a bun, a banana and chocolate at the Post Office/shop and went on up the hill to the next footpath. After four fields with two gates to climb, the path ended with a fence and a hedge and no stile or way at all. Oh dear, that meant going back through the fields and round by the lane. The next path was walkable and very pleasant, then the bridleway to Hatherleigh started as a well-used track from a farm, until past Medway, when it petered out in a field. I found a way across the stream then saw a small gate with a blue arrow and followed a muddy way between the trees. After another puzzling bit there were more blue arrows - thank goodness for the Explorer map! I'd have had problems trying to find the way with a Landranger in this area. Eventually the path reached another farm track leading to the road near Hatherleigh.

On reaching the main street and a telephone I tried to phone Dad (no reply) then phoned Anita, then went to the shop for a few food requirements, followed by a visit to the Acorn Tearooms for a cream tea with the two biggest scones I have ever seen and four cups of tea.

I bought a postcard and posted one to Malcolm then I followed the Tarka Trail and enjoyed views of Dartmoor soon after leaving Hatherleigh. Yes Tor and High Willhays were visible. I continued SE to Terris Bridge, where I left the Tarka Trail to follow the lane to Exbourne, where I asked a man as I entered the village if there was a likely farm where they might let me camp. I'm now pitched at the farm, Court Barton, near the church. The kind man here came out with a cup of tea and a slice of cake, also some water in plastic milk bottles, as he didn't trust my waterbag to do the job! "Don't you want it in containers?" he had asked me when I had first arrived and asked about water. After that tea and cake, on top of the cream tea, I was in no hurry to cook a meal so I put the food to soak while I went down the track to find out the time of the church service tomorrow (9am) and then phoned Dad from down in the village. I returned to cook the meal - no room for pudding of course - then I phoned Lynette and Rose. Now I'll go to the house for a wash, as they offered use of the bathroom up to 11pm. This was very welcome.

Today the lanes were full of daffodils and primroses; the trees were full of chaffinches and blackbirds. There was still a coldish east wind but it has been a lovely sunny day with views of Yes Tor, High Willhays and Cosdon Hill, bringing back memories of going there with Rusty a few years ago. (Rusty was our well-loved family dog, a collie cross, 1979-1996). Another enjoyable day of 14½ miles.

Sunday 16th March
- Exbourne to Chenson Camping Barn:

I woke at ten minutes to seven to hear rooks cawing and a dog barking. I'd heard it howling, singing, in the night but I slept all right. After breakfast I went in for a wash at 8am, having been told that the bathroom would be vacant then. I packed all except the flysheet so that the condensation could dry in the sun while I went across the road to reach the church by 8.55am - the church clock is 2 minutes slow. A few other people appeared then I heard some discussion about 9am or 9.30, and what "he" said and at which he church "he" would be at various times - apparently it was in the church mag (The Parish Pump) as 9.30am, and 9.30 it was. The four hymns were: Lead us, Heavenly Father, Lead us, We love the place O God, Forty days and forty nights, and Love Divine. Afterwards a kind lady, Sarah Horton, asked me back to their house, Copper Beeches, which I'd passed yesterday, for coffee - and toast and local honey! They also signed my sponsor form, donating £4, and I finally started walking at 11.30am, first going back to take a photo of the church, which I had forgotten to do before we left. Quiet, sunny lanes with primroses, daffodils and periwinkles soon took me to Bondleigh, the 5½ miles taking one hour and fifty minutes. I stopped here on the wide grass verge for lunch then took a photo of a thatched cottage, church and tree, the general village scene. A path almost opposite the church via some gardens led down to the River Taw and back to the Tarka Trail. At first the route was through riverside fields, then a lane and a path to the ruins of Wood Farm, with views across the valley to the hilltop village of Coldridge, then on along a woodland path until eventually I came down to the railway and road with the steep lane up to Chenson Camping Barn.

What a big place for one person! I unpacked, looked to see what pans there were - only one apart from frying pans - put my dehydrated liver and onions, leek and runner beans to soak, then made soup and tea, cooked and ate my meal, also apple and cherry crumble and custard and more tea, then washed up and had a shower - you go outside and in the next door for the showers. Next I tried to remember what photos I had taken since the beginning of the walk; I should have written them down each day. Today was 11½ miles, not bad for a late start, a total of 175½ so far. It was beautifully sunny and spring-like all day. Now for bed, downstairs on a bench with the unpacked flysheet under the sleeping bag for extra comfort; the floor upstairs seems too hard and bare. Today's flowers included Dog's mercury and, as in Cornwall, the round leaves of pennywort on walls everywhere.

Monday 17th March
- Chenson Camping Barn to Bishop's Nympton:
It was surprising how long it took to pack. Food went in the bottom of the rucksack, then clothing and everything else (I'd had to unpack the tent of course, to get to other items) then I collected the water bottle from the kitchen and checked that I'd left nothing anywhere then I went round to the house to get my LEJOG form signed. I was glad to get out of the cold barn into the warm sun; the barn faced north with one small window on the east end, which got no sun, the hill behind being in the way, and there was quite a gap under the door. Before I went out I had taken a photo of a hen looking in at the glass-panelled door. Was she used to people feeding her?

Now I was off on a sunny bridleway across the hilltop field to a lane and on to Chawleigh to post off maps at the Post Office and buy a postcard. Today's route went up hills with the sun on my back, and down again. The lanes were lined with celandines and primroses, and fading snowdrops. At one point the sound of a hunting horn drifted across the fields twice, a sound going back for hundreds of years, but I saw nothing. Buzzards were about again, mewing in the sky, and in the trees chaffinches, blackbirds and a wren. Eventually I came to Odam Hill via a little-used bridleway and stopped for a drink of water. A passing farmer stopped his vehicle to tell me the way: "Turn off right, back there...." but that was the way I'd come! From Mariansleigh a footpath left a farm, going downhill between banks and brambles, slow but not difficult, then across fields to Park Farm and the lane to Bishop's Nympton, reaching the village just as the church clock struck five. It took another half hour to reach Jean's at Slough Farm. How nice to arrive! After the heat of the day a wash and change was what I wanted most. It was lovely to see Jean and Arthur and have a meal with them. Auntie Alice, Wendy and Derek came up during the evening, and Derek kindly left his mobile phone charger for me to use overnight. That was much appreciated. We had a pleasant evening. My food parcel was also there, ready to unpack and sort out, which did not take too long as it was only a three-day parcel. I think it was 14 miles today, a day so warm that it really felt more like summer than spring.

Tuesday 18th March
- Bishop's Nympton to Dulverton, Northcombe Farm:
How strange to sleep in a bed! When I drew the curtains this morning there were no distant views - just mist and a rook in a tree. I packed the food from my food parcel and made use of the shampoo included in it and enjoyed a lovely breakfast cooked by Jean; Arthur had gone to work. I wasn't surprised to find that time had got on as we were talking, of course, so it must have been at least 10.15am when I started walking. Jean walked with me as far as Hayne Plantation then I climbed the stile and set off downward between the trees. At one point a deer crossed the track in front of me; I took a photo of the empty grassy area after it had vanished so that I could imagine it there. After going under the A361 I went up the track/footpath past South Hayne Farm then along quiet lanes eastward, coming on to the next map at Abbots Park, one mile south of Molland. At Lee a path cuts off a corner, passing through a farm where the farmer was carrying a week-old lamb. I took a photo of a ewe and lamb in the next field then continued through the gate to the lane to sit in the sun at the edge of some woodland for my lunch.

This is three miles west of East Anstey. Buzzards are calling; there have been buzzards and pheasants all morning. At East Anstey I suddenly decided to go into the churchyard before going on and looked at the names on the gravestones until I found James and Alice Maud Summers, my grandparents, who died in 1943 and 1966 respectively, under a tree with crocuses and primroses growing there. I took a photo and another of the church before going on to Oldways End, where I stopped to take a photo, have a drink of water and post a card. I continued eastward then down the Dulverton road as far as the track up Streamcombe. This track ascends gently between trees, then at Streamcombe a path leaves over an almost hidden stile, zig-zags between trees on an easy gradient then on over open sheep pastures to look down on Dulverton, where I was to meet Jim & Maggie Beed. Both distant and nearer hills were misty now, although it was still sunny where I was. I descended into Dulverton and went up past the church to the path to Northcombe Farm, arriving about 6pm. Jim had already arrived at the camping barn and told me that Maggie had had time off the previous week because her mother was ill so she was not able to come but had instructed him to take me out for a meal in Dulverton. Mollie greeted me at the barn door and Jim soon had some coffee and cake on the table. When I'd pitched the tent we went by car down to the Bridge Inn and enjoyed a meal.

I slept well that night, and warmly, so was surprised to see frost in the morning.

Wednesday 19th March
- Dulverton to Taunton:
Well, it was a fortnight ago that I started from Land's End. Again I started on a lovely sunny morning with Jim & Mollie, although the tent hadn't dried out when I packed. We had breakfast in the barn then left to go down the track and on to a hamlet called Bury with a ford and a lovely stone bridge, then up a bridleway, often walking in a streamlet, on upwards until we were on a dry, grassy way where we stopped under a tree for coffee. We went on up to the trig point amid burnt heather on Haddon Hill (355 metres). There was a hazy but lovely view. We continued above Wimbleball Lake through open woodland until we reached the B road at Upton, then it was another mile to the Lowtrow Inn, where we had a good pot of tea. Here we said goodbye, as Jim & Mollie had to return to Dulverton for the car to drive home. It had been nice to have their company and I was sorry that Maggie couldn't join us.

From here I turned right on the narrow lane for the bridleway to Sholford Farm. What an obstructed way! From barbed wire to an unusable rusty gate, then the woodland where it was so difficult to squeeze between the trees that I took an easier line than that of the map-path, emerging from the wood over a stream and deciding that it would be easier to head for Winters, a farm that I could see across a couple fields. Had I seen anyone I would have explained why, but nobody was about. At Huish Champflower another path could not be found (somebody's garden appeared to be on its line); this meant another detour by road, but from Maundown I found the bridleway over the hill to Wiveliscombe and very pleasant it was. I was delighted to be off the road. After another path above the old railway, across fields and down to the road, I thought I'd better continue to Milverton by road, as paths shown on the map were not signposted or visible on the ground; time was getting on and daylight had to be considered. Past Milverton at Houndsmoor I phoned Margaret and said that I'd continue walking until it was dark. Drinks of water and squares of chocolate sustained me at a fair pace along narrow lanes, with another time-wasting (15minutes) attempt at a footpath over a golf course, until I reached Hillfarance and the lane to Allerford. An Explorer map might have helped here.

As I turned a corner of lane it really seemed to get darker suddenly - after all it was 7 o'clock - so I stopped where the lane was wider and got out the mobile phone to tell Malcolm where I was. He picked me up at a farm near a footpath and will return me to that point tomorrow. It was nice to enjoy a meal with them, then a leisurely bath and cut toenails, then a very pleasant and relaxed evening looking at maps and phoning Dad. We also discussed a possible campsite for Thursday as I hadn't decided just where I should camp. I slept well, too tired after 20 miles walking, and talking of course, to write the diary until after 7am on Thursday. Now it is time to get up!

Thursday 20th March 2003
- Taunton to Bowden's Campsite near Langport:

I had thought last night that I had no blisters after that long road walk, but on getting out of bed this morning I felt a tiny one, less than a quarter inch across, under my left big toe. It felt all right with socks on so I did nothing to it. Malcolm dropped me off at 9.30am at the farm where he had picked me up last night. I had the pleasure of grass underfoot for an hour to Silk Mills Road, Taunton, then on across fields until I had to use roads (Malcolm had told me which) to proceed through Taunton to the canal road, buying a pint of milk at a shop on the way. At the canal I sat in warm sunshine to turn over the map and eat an apple. I'd already had a drink of the fresh cold milk. By the River Tone there had been several wrens singing and I saw the blue flowers of speedwell, and here, growing on the bridge, is the first white dead nettle of the year. I follow the Bridge-water and Taunton canal via Creech St Michael to Charlton.

At Creech St Michael I stopped at a picnic table for lunch with my feet airing in the sun. Just before that a man doing surveying along the canal asked about the walk. Stitchwort and coltsfoot grew along the canal banks. The many vociferous wrens near Taunton had given way to chiff-chaffs, blackbirds, and chaffinches; the canal was home to moorhen and mallard. The moorhens usually hurried with a squawk to the far side while the mallards either lazed on the bank or chased the females up and down the canal. The poor ducks were well outnumbered by the drakes, whose green heads shone in the sun.

At Charlton I left the canal over the railway bridge to return to green pastures beside the River Tone, which was wider here. Flat lands stretched away as I walked the flood bank, strewn with debris from high waters. Later on a fair number of swans appeared, mostly standing in a field, but when I and two dog-walkers coming from the other direction came along, the nearer ones took flight with a whirr of large wings. Apart from one curlew they were the only birds I saw along here. I stopped and sat in the warm sunshine for a "socks off" break. I was interested to see beehive shaped stooks of reeds, apparently drying for use in thatching. There were several groups of them. These miles on grass were easy underfoot but were followed by road at Stoke St Gregory, where I saw the first violets of the year along the hedge bank. This lane took me to Stathe where I joined the Parrett Trail for another riverside walk on the grassy flood bank, until I reached the drove over the bridge, leading to Aller.

I was feeling ready to stop soon, but the air was cooler. I had to ask a lady where the path up the hill started, as there was no sign. It was only a few yards away, steep but not too tiring at the end of the day. A stile brought me to levelish fields and woods then I went through to the lane to find the campsite (Bowdens) arriving at ten to seven, dusk. It was £3 a night including hot water and showers, plus 20p for a duck egg from their own ducks. I pitched the tent and tucked into dehydrated chicken & vegetable soup, macaroni cheese with broccoli and leek then banana custard, and tea, of course. Af-ter a wash - just what the feet wanted - I was ready to settle down at 9.30pm after another 20-mile day. At first a noisy radio or television from a caravan kept me awake, but not for long. Unfortunately there was the same disturbance at six in the morning then I slept until 7 o'clock, to find early mists but peace and quiet.

Friday 21st March 2003
- Bowden's Campsite near Langport, via Glastonbury, to The Pheasant Inn, Wookey:

That was a good campsite: plenty of facilities for £3, and a shop as well. The duck egg, 20p, from their own ducks, I had for breakfast, with toast that I'd carried from the beginning. I washed my thick socks this morning, then eventually left at 9.40 after getting my LEJOG form signed. Three miles of lanes took me to the northern edge of the Taunton map, past Low Ham. So at "44" I walked on to the next map near Pitney Steart Bridge, this time arriving in sunshine, compared with last October's visit in rain. I knew what the drove was like, having walked it in October - an hour's walk - and I knew what the bridleway across the lane was like (overgrown with deep ruts and a stream running down it) - so didn't use it. I tried the footpath marked on the map but had to go under wire and through the hedge to the top field. There were no signs at the top or bottom of the footpath and I had to climb a gate to get out at the top. However, there was a sign and stile opposite for the path down towards Walton - good! I was at the shop/PO by one o'clock and bought a postcard, sausage roll and a banana - I already had a tomato.

Now I went on through Walton and down the lane as far as a bridge where I turned right towards Glastonbury at a sign, stopping here for lunch at 1.30pm. I'd felt a twinge in my thigh as I turned on to either a wheel rut or cattle rut, but expected it to vanish after a rest. Unfortunately this path was very obstructed, each gate having to be climbed, also having a strand of electric fence to go over/ under before and after each gate. As I approached Glastonbury a factory filled the view so I did not take a photo. I bought some postcards, found a tearoom, and sat down for a pot of tea and scone with jam. Delicious.

When I stood up - Ouch! When I walked - Ouch! I found a sort of hobble with weight on the poles and proceeded at this strange pace for a few miles in the direction of Wookey. I was going to meet other backpackers there for a Club weekend. From one footpath I took a photo back towards Glastonbury Tor, then continued to another lane. The man who had been surveying the canal appeared on his bike and gave some encouragement. It seemed that from now on it would be road to Wookey as footpaths seemed to be non-existent and non-signed. I hobbled on. Always the first step on the left leg was most painful, then easier once I was moving. At least I had two poles to help take the weight.

As dusk drew nearer I realised that I shouldn't get to the campsite in daylight (or in any sort of comfort); I phoned Tony Wilson for Dave Britton's mobile number to contact him. At last, in darkness, I gratefully sat down at a picnic table outside the Pheasant Inn at Wookey, and phoned Dave, who had arranged the weekend, to say where I was and that I could go no further. He said that he and the other Club members would join me there and enquired if they served food. Yes, they did. I went in and ordered some home-made soup and a drink of water and sat with my foot up, where the others soon trooped in and found me. Julia asked for some ice for my leg and we had a pleasant evening there.

Back at the campsite the other backpackers kindly pitched my tent while I sat in Dave's car and Dave brought a thick down jacket to use as a pillow for extra comfort, while Julia produced a painkiller and I was soon asleep.

Saturday 22nd March
- Wookey via Wells to the Priddy Road, Mendips:
I had a good night but putting weight on the left leg in the morning was still painful. What an advantage to have Julia, a physiotherapist, with us. She felt my leg in the morning and said it was probably the flexor tendon that I'd pulled - probably the rough ground and the stiles, meaning the gate-climbing near Glastonbury. She gave me some Neurofen tablets and offered some Arnica ointment, which I already had, and recommended an easy day, followed by up to ten miles tomorrow and more easy days. The other backpackers departed for their walk, leaving Lynette to transport me to "connect up" at the Pheasant at Wookey, where I'd finished walking last night, and to take my rucksack in her car, God bless her, and she stopped perhaps every mile or so for me to rest in the car and have a drink of water. I walked/hobbled about two miles to Wells, I think, where we stopped (met up when Lynette had parked her car) by the Cathedral, where we sat in the spring sunshine and enjoyed the pork and salad baguettes she'd brought

from Chard and the apples I'd bought, then I tried to phone Dad from three phone boxes with no success and we had a pot of tea before we continued in the same manner. Julia recommended road walking, not rough ground, to avoid further twinges, so Lynette and I agreed on various stopping points where she'd wait for me then I'd have a drink of water and a rest.

I tried one more phone box on the way out of Wells, found the line still engaged so phoned Anita, saying that I thought Dad's receiver must be not quite on properly, (I was concerned about him, at nearly 92 years old, and he liked to be kept up-to-date with my progress) so Anita kindly said she'd try phoning him later, then would go round in the evening when they went out, so that put my mind at rest. When we reached the lane leading to Priddy I'd done seven miles and thought I'd better not risk any more that day. First Lynette drove us to her daughter, Catherine's at Chewton Mendip for a cup of tea, then on to Bath Youth Hostel, where we were booked in for the night.

The Backpackers, especially Lynette, had been very good to me. I phoned Trevor and Maurice (my sons) to tell them that I shouldn't make Saltford next day, where we were to have met at The Jolly Sailor for a pub lunch, but I would phone to let them know where to meet for lunch, depending on my progress. I found the standing and hobbling about the kitchen hard on my leg but enjoyed my meal of soup then turkey in parsley sauce with red pepper, runner beans, carrot and mash then peach crumble and custard. We were ready for bed quite early so I had a shower, washed socks and underwear and settled down before 10pm I think; fortunately there was a lower bunk available for me and I slept well after a happy, satisfying day.

Sunday 23rd March
- Priddy Road, Mendips, to Clutton Hill:

We woke at about 6am and probably got up about 6.30-7am. I was able to get out of bed and onto my feet quite comfortably. I washed my hair and my green T-shirt. It seemed a little easier coming downstairs this morning and Lynette and I enjoyed our breakfast (Porridge, Yeo valley yoghurt and a banana and tea). I was able to move about the kitchen without the use of my poles. Outside, as we were leaving, a cyclist was pumping up a tyre so I asked if he'd take a photo of Lynette and myself on the steps. Then we returned to where I'd stopped walking yesterday at the Priddy lane and I started walking at 9.45am when we'd discussed the route and stops. We did the same routine of Lynette taking the rucksack in her car while I hobbled along watching for flowers in the hedgerows until I saw Lynette's car ahead again.

What a delightful spring day again! Today's bird was the chiff-chaff. Besides primroses, celandines and violets, a new spring flower today was the wood anemone, and I've just remembered that a few days ago in Devon I saw the flowers of barren strawberry.

Point 186 on the Bristol and Bath Landranger map was a point where I met up with Lynette, and here I phoned Trevor and Nicky at ten past eleven and said that I expected to reach Hinton Blewett in an hour, explaining where the village was and that there was a PH marked on the map there. Lynette would arrive before me so I told her to look out for Trevor's and Nicky's blue car and four young people and tell them that I'd be there soon. I found them at a table outside the Ring O'Bells with Lynette, waving to me across the green. It was lovely to see them all.

Most of us had various salads for lunch (Maurice and Lynette had soup) but the size of my three-cheese salad was tremendous! There were three chunks of about ¼ lb each, or more, and in spite of offering it around and eating as much as I could, I still packed away enough for three days' packed lunches. I really should have asked Lynette to take a photo of us with the large platefuls in front of us but we were concentrating so much on eating it! She took a photo of Maurice, Julie, Trevor, Nicky and me at the table with the empty glasses, then I took one of her outside the door, and thanked her for being my "guardian angel" then she made her way to visit another of her family while Trevor took my rucksack and Maurice and Trevor drove to Temple Cloud while Julie and Nicky walked with me along the leafy, flowery lanes.

We saw goldfinches, chaffinches and a buzzard - the buzzard was later when we were all together near Clutton. I found walking uphill much easier than the downhill slopes. Later Maurice and Trevor parked their cars at Clutton Hill and walked back to join us. We walked on up the lane to the Clutton 1 mile sign, where I took a photo of the four of them, then went back to the cars. I lightened my load by giving Trevor and Nicky the milk powder and meths to bring to me later, which they had offered to do, then I took my rucksack, waved as they drove off, and headed for the bridleway down the road. On the right of the bridleway a man and a girl were seeing to some horses in a yard. I asked about camping and the man said I could go anywhere in the field and showed me the water tap. I pitched and cooked a meal, then I heard a voice: "The kettle's just boiled. Make yourself some tea. We'll leave the electricity on so use the electric kettle when you want." Kind people again. The man had said that I should leave in the morning by walking up the field to a gate or stile onto the bridleway as the Shire horses would be loose in the yard.

What a lovely, enjoyable day. I settled comfortably with my cup of tea, food for the meal soaking, then I phoned Trev to say how I'd got on, then Anne Ling to update her with the news, then had my meal, washed up, washed self and clothes. I lit the candle, made Ovaltine and wrote the diary, thinking what lovely family and friends I have, and pleasant places to camp. I had stopped at five o'clock and when I'd pitched the sun shone into my tent and I enjoyed its warmth. It wasn't dark until seven o'clock. Contentment, and no pain now!

Monday 24th March
- Clutton Hill to Cold Ashton (and Cotswold Way):

I heard owls last night, and this morning the whinny of a horse and the nearby call of a pheasant. When the sun appeared from behind a cloud I unzipped the east side of the tent, moved the stove across and had breakfast in the sun. I'd been over to the electric kettle at the stables and made mug of tea then brought water back to boil my egg and wash up. I finished my film with a photo of the tent, packed then set off at 9.30am, taking a photo of the Shire horses in the yard before I left. They plodded contentedly about the yard munching hay now and then. All was peaceful. I made my way up the field and out under a gate with a large gap to the stony bridleway. I soon heard the calls of lapwings, which surprised me, in a field to my left, then above the next field skylarks were singing. The only flowers here were dandelions and daisies. After the first burst of sunshine the sky clouded over but it was till dry and warm. Now there is a yellowhammer in the hedge as I pause to write this beside the lane past the New Inn (PH on A39). As I continued along lanes to Stanton Prior the flora increased - dog's mercury, celandines, primroses, and violets, mostly white ones.

At Stanton Prior I took a photo of some black and white calves in a farmyard with lovely old buildings - more new life - then I made use of the phone box to phone Joyce Griffith with the latest news of LEJOG. It was nice to have a chat with her. Going down the lane into Saltford was hard on the legs, then I had a short break from the pack weight when I stopped at the shops to buy 4 stamps, a small bar of Bournville chocolate, an apple and a tomato, then I continued down to the River Avon, using a short stretch of the Avon Walkway to cross it. Now a mile of level field paths led to the A431 (Bristol to Bath). Here two swans flew over; I love the sound of their wing beats. The grass was green and soft underfoot. Two canoeists paddled rhythmically by. On the other side of the A431 a lane climbs steeply, which eased my legs and I was able to keep up a steady pace to North Stoke, then had a sit down and drink of water beside the bridleway, hearing sheep and lambs all around. I'd heard chiffchaffs and green woodpeckers, as I'd come down to Saltford.

Soon there was a Cotswold Way signpost, beginning another stage of the journey. The way climbed gently on a stony track to Pipley Wood then I continued on the bridleway through the next wood to reach the road and give a more even surface for my leg. It was just over a mile to Lower Hamswell where I rejoined the Cotswold Way over easy grass, then it was a long mile uphill towards dusk to reach Cold Ashton in the dark (about 7.30pm?) and, eventually, The Chestnuts, where I hoped to camp. The kind lady didn't charge (£3) as I'm doing it for charity. It seems that Bryan and Ron (two men, she said), stopped here two nights ago. I was soon pitched and tucking in to a mug of tea and a meal. The chickpeas, rice, parsley sauce and spring cabbage seemed the heaviest choice of meal to reduce the weight carried. I also had garlic and mushroom soup with the rice. Washing up followed, then washing self and clothes, by which time I was ready for sleep. A satisfying day of 14 miles.

Tuesday 25ᵗʰ March 2003
- Cold Ashton to Hawkesbury Upton:

I woke at ten to six to hear the cheerful tones of a songthrush. Other birds joined in now and then but the thrush was the soloist for some time. I just lay there enjoying it. When I decided at last to get up and unzip the tent there was thick mist. I listened to the news and weather at 7.30 and it seems that the mist will still be about until midmorning in the South-west. Never mind; I shall enjoy what I see and hear.

As I left Cold Ashton by the church path I took a photo of the signpost and daffodils, wanting some record of where I had been even in the mist. I could smell the turnip plants in a field, smell muck spreading in other fields and, in the wood, the smell of wild garlic. This was a delightful path, all too short, with golden saxifrage and dog's mercury and the green of bluebell leaves. I heard another green woodpecker and wood pigeons. The path passed through fields again, now in sunshine at 10.40, to Dyrham Park, which it skirted on a bridleway to a lane, then more fields, where bird's eye speedwell was the only flower, then beside a wood to a picnic site beside the M4, which was invisible but noisy. What a lot of litter on the approach to the picnic site. Why can't people use bins or take it home?

I had an early lunch of cheese, tomato and oatcakes, then I phoned Lynette to thank her for her help and to report on my progress. Now I went on via field paths with very difficult stiles, really awkward to climb on to and down from, to Old Sodbury, where I had to ask where the Post Office/shop was, as I couldn't see it - it was down the road. I had a rest on the seat at the crossroads, boots and socks off, then I went down to the shop for 2 rolls, 1 banana and 2 eggs. That is another helpful shop that will sell them in twos thus saving me extra weight to carry! I set off again to Little Sodbury where I took a photo of the church and paused to sit down by the churchyard wall for a drink of water and to write my diary while wood pigeons cooed and a blackbird sang.

Along the lane from here I asked an elderly couple what they were looking at with binoculars, expecting it to be an interesting bird. "Waymarks," they said, "We're checking waymarks on local footpaths." They asked where I was walking and I mentioned the difficult stiles after Tormarton. They said it was the landowner at Dodington House, but something would be done about them. Down the lane the path to the right was a streak of bright green leading to woodland where woodpeckers knocked on trees. A buzzard mewed. I entered the wood to ascend on a path through a carpet of wild garlic - that delicious smell again. Still woodpeckers pecked. It was so peaceful here that at the top I sat under a beech tree for a drink of water and to relax and just enjoy being there as the sun edged into a bank of mist behind the trees. The next bit was lane to Hawkesbury Upton. Why are Gloucestershire lanes so devoid of spring flowers? There were celandines, daisies, dandelions, the leaves of cow parsley but no primroses as in previous counties. However, the Gloucestershire woodlands are beautiful, really lovely. As dusk fell at ten to seven I walked up to Coombe Farm and asked to camp for the night. It was £3 for just cold water and a sheep trodden field corner.

In the night a barn owl screeched nearby, then more distantly. In the morning pheasants were near. At ten to seven the sun was shining and sheep wandered past. After three weeks of walking I've reached 309 miles.

Wednesday 26th March 2003
- Hawkesbury Upton to Nympsfield, Rose & Crown:

I had breakfast in the sun, changing my open zip from the lower east one to the upper east one as the sun moved round. After my porridge I enjoyed a delicious large brown egg and a roll, with butter left from Sunday's meal. The washing and my towel soon dried and I was off at 9.15, pleased to see that another wood, Splatt's Wood, was ahead. As the Way dropped into the wood I was really cheered to see primroses once more, and violets, wood anemones and hart's tongue fern. They were in the shade so I didn't take a photo until I came to some primroses where the valley opened out below the wood.

A buzzard soared across, rooks cawed and chiffchaffs did that, with the usual pheasant making itself heard. Two horses and riders passed. As I approached the lane larks were singing. What's the bird that whistles, "Veni, vidi, vici"? - I have heard it on two or three occasions but not seen it. On the next bridleway contouring Winner Hill I saw a solitary long tailed tit, and then a kestrel hovering only about 15 feet above the ground. As I watched, it flew to the top of a small tree very close to me, but I couldn't expect its sharp sight to miss my hand moving for the camera! It flew off of course. A cattle trough provided welcome water, by raising the lid and lifting the ball-cock while holding my mug under the inlet.

Now down at Alderley I paused to read the local notice board and laughed aloud on reading that one of the churchwardens was called Chris Summers! (my maiden name). Another bridleway brought me to a bridge over a stream. I stopped beside the stream in a patch of sunshine to rest my leg, have a banana and write this. An old barn is higher up the field, woods above that and blue sky above the woods. A wren is singing in a tree beside the clear water. I went on again, across the field, over a high stile, across the lane where an easy stile led to a path sloping up through woodland with banks of celandines. Higher up were hart's tongue fern, ivy and violets on steeper shady banks, then a difficult, rocky bit of path demanded concentration before the gradient eased with more open woodland and a few primroses then the track levelled out and I went on for a few minutes before stopping for lunch - this was the last of Sunday's cheese!

The long barrow marked on the map was invisible behind trees. The track led to a lane, which I'd decided to take to ease my leg. Julia had recommended road as opposed to rough going, so I continued by road between large fields with hardly a habitation to be seen. As I walked I considered tonight's pitch. It had to be found easily by Trevor and Nicky, who were bringing my things, so the village of Nympsfield seemed the best place to try. I'd made good time so far and asked at a house where there was a man in the garden who was very helpful. He suggested the pub, which had a small field behind, or if not, Pam the milk lady who lived up the track to the left of the pub, although she might have calves in her field, or if I had no luck there he had land on the other side of the village and buildings with water and a toilet.

The Rose and Crown was open and was just the job, with a field behind to camp in, a water tap outside, and easy for Trevor and Nicky to find. I pitched at about half past five and went down to the phone at about six o'clock to tell them how to get here, also to phone Dad, and on the way back, Richard, the man I'd asked in his garden, passed on the way to his farm and asked if I had found somewhere. Nice people.

I had to be quick soaking my turkey, broccoli, carrots and runner beans in order to finish my meal by 7.30 to meet Trevor and Nicky in the pub. I just managed it, washing up too. It was lovely to see them. They'd had a leak in their kitchen and the plumbers in so it was not a good day for them. They and I left about 9pm, the landlord not wanting payment for pitching. I waved off Trevor and Nicky and returned to the tent to do my washing - it was thick-socks-day (thin socks were washed every night but thick ones about every four days) - then I settled down to sleep at half past nine after another good day.

Thursday 27th March 2003
- Nympsfield via King's Stanley to Witcombe, near Cheltenham:

I slept well, waking at about 6.45am to hear a few birds and some traffic noise, but not too near. I had porridge then beans with the toast that Trevor and Nicky had brought, and then I finished writing yesterday's diary. It was a lovely sunny morning.

The lane took me to the road near Coaley Peak then across to the Peak, where views were very hazy. A load of soil had been spread so that I could not see the path nor the PCs shown here on the map so this wasted a bit of time (no PCs either; they were closed) but I was soon enjoying walking along soft woodland paths, gently up and down, with a few wood anemones and sunlight streaming between the bare branches and trunks, which was really lovely; there was the odd violet too. They were mostly beech trees in this wood, then out in the open a hawthorn hedge was bursting into leaf so I ate a few young leaves.

Eventually the Way descended to King's Stanley, where the phone wasn't working - you could see the loose wires - so I went on through the village, coming to a lovely old shop, F.HOLLEY & SONS. In I went, to pick up an apple, tomato and banana, wait for others to be served then I added strawberry yoghurt. As I was packing them in my rucksack at the gate one of the shop ladies came out for a chat about where I had been and asked if I'd like coffee. I thanked her and said I'd prefer water then she asked if I'd like to sit in their garden next door to have it - water with a drop of lemon in and a lovely slice of fruitcake (Simnel cake). What kind people I meet. Afterwards I went and thanked her and said she'd be mentioned in my diary - both ladies - so here they are!

After that welcome refreshment I went on in the heat and was glad to get to the railway footbridge and sit down on the grass before going up through fields then I diverted to a phone box to speak to Anne Ling and Dave Peachey about the weekend that Dave had arranged, camping at his uncle's farm at Ebrington, as I didn't think I'd be likely to make it. This took some time so I decided to use the lane to Randwick Church to get to Standish Woods. Again I enjoyed the woodland walking and the wood anemones under the trees. There were many other paths as well as the Cotswold Way. I left the wood for a bit of road walking then paths down to Painswick, but this downhill stretch was a strain on the legs, especially where there were some loose stones where the path descends towards a foot-bridge, so I planned to phone Liz and Dave from the phone box in Painswick, just out of the town, where Golf Course Road leaves the B road....but that phone box, too, was out of order so I had to use the mobile phone. I said I'd continue along the lane, which I did, to where it joined the main road and here Dave picked me up. As well as the long downhill bit the loose stones above the footbridge had been troublesome to the leg so, although it was a good start to the day, it was a hard finish after only 12 miles, the mile down to Pains-wick seeming like the longest mile I'd ever walked. However, it was nice to arrive to a good meal and pleasant company, followed by a hot bath. I hope the leg improves; it was doing well this morning. Now for a night in a comfortable bed - but that certainly doesn't mean that the Z-rest in the tent is not comfortable!

Friday 28ᵗʰ March 2003
- Witcombe to Shab Hill:

At 6.15am I could see out of the open window and hear green woodpeckers and pheasants, so with the daylight to wake me and the wildlife and fresh air it was almost like being in the tent. The leg isn't as good as I had expected but it is better than it was last night. Liz gave me a lovely breakfast then, after talking for a while, it must have been about quarter past ten when she dropped me at the end of Golf Course Road where I had finished last night. I set off along the road at first to ease into walking with a heavy pack and did not find too much traffic. The signpost to Cranham and Birdlip was welcome, as was a rest when I turned off the road. This was only after about two miles walking but my leg needed it. Here was plenty of wood-land again, the feature of Gloucestershire that I have most enjoyed - after all, it has been too hazy and misty for distant views. Dave and Liz say that you can see Hay Bluff, 40 miles away, from their house on a clear day.

The woodland birds seemed quiet today, but for a bursting black-bird or the cooing of woodpigeons and the occasional knocking of a woodpecker. Small birds were not much in evidence, although I did hear the "Veni, vidi, vici" bird and one with a repetitive whistle, and I heard a buzzard mewing over open hillside to my left. The flowers were wood anemones and a few violets, with young shoots of nettles and bluebell leaves greening the ground. The woodland track of the Cotswold Way had the usual horseshoe imprints but the dry weather made it mud-free. Some trees were marked with a horseshoe waymark, indicating a riding route. I'd seen two horses when I'd sat down after leaving the main A46 (Stroud) road.

I stopped early for lunch, about 12 o'clock, so as to have less weight to carry, but after this break my stops became more frequent as the leg discomfort increased. When I came to Barrow Wake I could see Oakland Farm across the valley but it was much too misty for a photo, which would have appeared all grey-green. I decided to use the lane going under the A417 heading north-east then the one going south-east to Coberley for easier walking, and from there I thought I'd rejoin the Cotswold Way at Upper Coberley. However, I was now needing to stop every 15 minutes at the most and was stiff each time I restarted so, reluctantly, at half past three I phoned Dave on the mobile phone and asked if he could pick me up - a hard decision but a sensible one I think. Dave and Liz are lovely kind people whose help merely in taking a food parcel would have been welcome, but in my difficulties their assistance has been marvellous.

Saturday 29th March 2003:
Daylight. A pheasant call. Stretch leg in bed, bend, stretch. Still some discomfort, even lying down. I dozed off until twenty to eight. I could stand, and walk with a limp. I phoned Maurice to ask him not to pick me up and take the rucksack after all, having phoned Julia for advice, which was to go home for a week's rest and get it X-rayed if there was no improvement. After breakfast I phoned for train times: 12.12 from Cheltenham. Next I phoned Dad, then Anita, who suggested Bob Wharne for a lift from Crewe Station since she was leaving for Bedfordshire. Dave kindly took me Cheltenham Spa Station and the journey passed quickly. Bob and June met me and took me to Kwik Save to do some shopping before taking me home, which was very good of them. I hope I'll soon be able to walk again. It seems very strange being here when my mind is still in the Gloucestershire woodland with the birds singing.

Monday 31st March:
No improvement - still painful - so I phoned Anita to ask if she could take me to Leighton Hospital tomorrow, early.

Tuesday 1st April: No April Fool's Joke
- It is a Fracture.

Anita took me to A & E between 9 and 9.30am. After the X-ray I was kept waiting on a trolley; they had no one to return me or to tell Anita where I was. Then I was wheeled back to A & E and Anita eventually found me reading a magazine. When the doctor saw me and the X-ray he told me that it was a stress fracture to the neck of the femur, that I should have two cannulated screws put in and that I'd get back 95% of my walking ability. That was all quite a shock but 95% sounded all right. I was sent up to the Orthopaedic Blue ward and Anita, bless her, went home with a list of things I'd need. I was to have nothing to eat or drink in case the operation was that day, but by early evening it was obviously not going to happen and at last I had a sandwich and drink of water and later a cup of tea. In this part of the ward there are two Christines and two Marys! I had a visit from Rex with a Get Well card, which was a photo of Dibley (their dog that I often walk).

Wednesday 2nd April: Screws in!

No breakfast of course, but there was not long to wait for the trolley to take me down. Someone asked if I was nervous but I said No, I wanted to get it over. When it *was* over I was told that the operation took an hour and three quarters. I could have had an epidural but just imagine being aware of people sawing and drilling away at your bones for all that time even if you couldn't feel it! I think I dozed, on and off, for the rest of the day, attempted to eat a delicious pork casserole meal but couldn't manage much of it, then fruit salad, which I did manage, and I tried to concentrate on reading - I'd asked Anita to bring Lonesome Heights (by Halliwell Sutcliffe) in for me. I really enjoyed reading this.

Thursday 3rd April
- Monday 7th April: Cards and Crutches

These days passed surprisingly quickly, with the pleasant company of the other ladies - two Marys and another Christine! - until two of us were moved to another bay on Saturday. We chose meals from the menu - not bad meals - and enjoyed receiving cards and visitors. Anita kindly brought Dad and I asked her to take a photo of me in hospital to help use up the film. The worst time was being told that I could put no weight on the leg for 6 weeks so thoughts of resuming LEJOG soon were shattered, and of finding that I couldn't get anywhere trying to use a frame to walk - fortunately a kind student nurse, Julie, suggested that I go straight on to crutches, which I immediately felt more at home with and was soon doing well with them. It was also sad to read my name in TGO with Bryan's and Ron's, saying that we were walking LEJOG, so I tried to concentrate on the good things, like the visitors and increasing number of Get Well cards including Tony Wilson's card comprising photos taken on LEJOG at Coad's Green, Cornwall and Wookey, Somerset.

On the Friday I'd had a short practice on the stairs with the crutches, but about 8 stairs wasn't a lot - this was because I was told that I could go home on Monday if I could manage stairs on crutches and if someone could take a commode home for me (Stella did this).

Saturday 5th April: Family visit.
The best thing that happened today was when I'd crutched along the corridors to see off Dad, and Stella who'd brought him, then settled down again in the chair by the bed to read....I looked up and saw Trevor and Nicky, Maurice and Julie standing there smiling! What a lovely surprise and how kind of them to come all the way from Bristol and Weston-super-Mare to visit me in hospital! They brought me books and an Easter Egg (which I kept until Easter) but just to see them was lovely!

Monday 7th April: Home again!
I had another crutch practice on the Monday morning ready for going home on Monday afternoon. However, this practice was only up and down eight or nine stairs so I was not too sure about managing the stairs at home. I could nip around the ward and corridors quite confidently. I said goodbye to the other patients and the kind nurses, especially Julie, then early in the afternoon the ambulance came and I was soon home to my bed in the dining room and some cheering flowers, which turned out to have been left by Katie, and a bit of freedom to do things, like cook a jacket potato and cheese for tea. I have to sleep on my back, unfortunately, so wake in the night with it aching, but read until sleep comes once more, then I wake to hear the birds singing.

Friday 30ᵗʰ May 2003: In a Tent!

There was a Backpackers Club static weekend at Biggin for the Tissington Well Dressings, arranged by Geoff Gadsby. Of course, I couldn't backpack, but if someone could give me a lift there I could sleep in the tent - bliss - and go by bus to Tissington and crutch back to Biggin. Lawrence and Lesley very kindly gave me a lift there and there were offers from Club members to pitch my tent behind the Waterloo Inn, but I said I would see how I got on and call for help if I couldn't manage on one leg and crutches. I managed, but someone kindly fetched water for me - that would have been difficult to carry on crutches. I didn't use the tent inner but had brought a groundsheet to use under the flysheet, giving me more room to move. I slept well, even on my back, on the Thermarest, the best night I'd had for weeks. Next morning a few of us caught a bus from outside the Waterloo Inn to Tissington, where I happily crutched around with the others then we stopped for a pot of tea and cake, sitting at a table outside. The Well Dressings had been excellent as usual in all their colourful variety. When we reached the Tissington Trail we met Peter Bellamy, from Coventry, stopped for a chat then continued steadily along. I had my folding stool over my shoulder so that I could sit down when I needed a rest. Once more I was enjoying the wild flowers beside the track. We stopped for lunch at a picnic area, then went on again, back to Biggin. Lawrence and Lesley were going home that night, which suited me - I had had a night in the tent and been with other Backpackers Club members and thoroughly enjoyed it.

Tuesday 23ʳᵈ June 2003: The bone has healed well

The check up at the hospital was today; I was told that the bone had healed well and that I could gradually come off the crutches, down to one crutch then no crutches when I felt confident. That was good news! - my next check-up is not until September. I did not see much point in using two crutches as I'd automatically let them take the weight so went straight down to using one. After that I tended to use one crutch when I went out and none about the house. At first going up stairs I found I had no "push" in my left leg, due to the muscles not being used all that time. It was the same when I started cycling again (in July) - no "push" in the left leg, but little by little the muscles improved and I could increase my walking distance. Once I was able to cycle again I pushed the bicycle to the cycle shop for a service then cycled home and that, I think, was the end of using the crutches.

Friday 20th June 2003: Coping with a train and crutching about.
Another Well Dressings Backpackers weekend. I managed to get to and from this one by train, coping with getting on and off the train on crutches, but camping both nights at Hope where the others joined us on Saturday evening. Even so, I managed to crutch for a good walk, carrying the folding stool for when I needed to sit down. Also in a shop at Hope I bought some Sorbothane heel pads, ready for when I start walking again. I'm sure they will help to prevent the jarring. In Hope I watched some of the preparations for the Well Dressing, where they were actually putting sprigs of parsley and heads of daisies into the display panels.

Friday 4th
- Sunday 6th July: Increasing distances.
I went up with Pat & Steve to the Saunders Lakeland Mountain Marathon, and helped at base camp for registration on the Friday, and at the mid-way camp on Saturday, and again at base camp on the Sunday, handing out meal tickets. Also on the Friday evening I'd crutch-walked up to Low Rigg, two miles each way, which was satisfying, even coping with stiles all right. Later in the month Jim and Maggie had kindly invited me down to Exmouth. I went by train and during the few days there I walked at least five miles per day with them, or one of them. This was progress indeed! How I enjoyed those walks!

Thursday 31st July
- Sunday 3rd August 2003: Back to Backpacking!
Next came the great milestone of my first proper Backpacking weekend. This was Cadair Idris from Arthog. I arrived by train on the Thursday afternoon and just had a short evening walk in the drizzle to break myself in. I did not plan to go up Cadair Idris but started with a day walk on the Friday, seven and a half miles over the hills to Castell y Bere near Abergynolwyn. I had not explored the twelfth century castle ruins before so found that interesting, and there was more to see than I had expected. If I had felt that I'd had enough I could have returned by train, using the Tal-y-Llyn railway to get down to Towyn, but I felt able to manage the seven and a half

miles back too, although I was glad to finish the downhill walking. Having walked 15 miles without carrying the tent, I decided that I'd be all right to backpack next day but I could just stop and pitch if I felt the need.

I walked with three others, stopping at an old farmhouse after seeing a sign for teas. We were served by a lovely old lady who told us that the doctor had said she could carry on doing this as long as she felt up to it. Then we followed the Pony Path up towards Cadair Idris, turning right at the top, where we stopped for a rest on some rocks, and to enjoy the view, and then following the ridge round before dropping to the track leading to the sheepfolds, beyond which we camped on a grassy area. A very satisfying day's walk! Next day was fine too and the return walk to Arthog was successfully completed over the hills and down past the waterfalls. I was absolutely delighted to be backpacking once more, and to have done it without any aches and pains.

Now the Backpackers Club weekends would continue to keep me fit over the next few months until I could eagerly continue LE-JOG from Witcombe, once more following the Spring north.

Sunday 7ᵗʰ March 2004: LEJOG
- Continuing at last!

Of course, I woke up feeling excited today! Anita and Paul took me to Crewe Station for the 3.08pm train - which was on time - and it seemed no time before it arrived at Cheltenham at 4.51pm. Dave Lee met me and took me back to Oakland Farm, Witcombe. It did seem a little strange going up the steps and walking into the house thinking, "I'm not in pain!" It was good to see Liz again and to chat with them both over a lovely meal and afterwards, and to see their photos of the Pennine Way. It certainly did not feel like a year since I'd left them, more like last month. I slept well.

Monday 8ᵗʰ March
- Shab Hill near Witcombe to Hailes Fruit Farm near Winchcombe:

Liz gave me a big breakfast and as I finished it Julia and Ros arrived to accompany me, with Stuart, who had brought them, and he then drove us to Shab Hill where I'd had to abandon the walk last March. He took a photo of the three of us, on his camera and mine, then went back while we walked on via the Gloucestershire

Way and Cowley to Seven Springs and rejoined the Cotswold Way over Wistley Hill and down to Dowdeswell reservoir, then steadily uphill with a pause on the way to cool down then on to the tops once more. It was lovely to be walking the Cotswolds again, and in good company.

The weather was mostly sunny with a few clouds and a cool breeze. Gloves were needed at first and again after lunch, also the woolly hat, but not all the time. We saw the first primroses and, just before Winchcombe, the first lambs in the fields. Our lunch stop was under the trees near Upper Hill farm after about 9 miles. We omitted the detour round Cleeve Hill to save distance on this first day, and made for Belas Knap, a long barrow, via the deserted Wontley Farm. Ros took a photo of Julia and myself at the entrance to Belas Knap, which resembles a smaller version of Barclodiad y Gawres on Anglesey. We descended, not too steeply, to Winchcombe through woodland at first then fields, all dry underfoot.

Winchcombe was attractive with its stone houses and small shops. Ros checked on bus times as we passed a timetable, because she and Julia had to get a bus back to Cheltenham and they realised that if they went on for the two miles to Hailes Fruit Farm with me then back to Winchcombe they'd miss the last bus, so they accompanied me to the lane or track leading to Hailes and left to catch the earlier bus. I thanked them for their good company and headed upward, stopping at a grassy corner for a drink of water, then on until the track reached a stile with the Cotswold Way arrow pointing into a field. An easy path led through fields to Hailes Abbey ruins (National Trust - not open until April) then up the lane to the fruit farm where I asked where to camp and was shown a green strip between the apple trees.

A few minutes later, as I was pitching the tent, I heard voices and saw that Anne, Dave Peachey and Dave Bennett had arrived. Dave Peachey had arranged a Club "weekend" on my route, as he did last year when I could not make it. It was good to see them. I put food to soak then had a shower, being glad of my "Caledonian Sleeper" shower mat on the concrete floor. While I was eating, Dave Bennett came over to say that instead of going to the pub (2 miles away) it might be a good idea to have an early night and an early start tomorrow for Ebrington. This also gave me time to write my diary during the evening. 15 miles - and a very good day!

Tuesday 9ᵗʰ March
- Hailes to Ebrington:

There were lots of tawny owls calling last night and a few this morning. I got up about 6.20am and had porridge and poached egg for breakfast then we set off at 8.15 after a cold but not frosty night. (I'd needed my thick socks on). The sun gave a little warmth where we were sheltered from the cold breeze. We passed Hailes Abbey ruins again (not open yet, gate padlocked, Nat. Trust owned and English Heritage administered). After a track through dry ploughland, green fields led towards woods then a track ascended steadily. We had a break where water pumps rhythmically but quietly worked away in the woods, and the Daves teased Anne that we'd taken a wrong turn and would have to go back! I took a photo, or one of the Daves did, of the three of us under the trees and later I took one looking back to Cleeve Hill, where Julia, Ros and I were yesterday. This woodland walk was lovely, although there were no spring flowers yet, but at Snowshill there were snowdrops, daffodils and aubrietia in the gardens. I took a photo of the church (and imagined the bells ringing!).

Dave and Dave had suggested omitting the drop to and climb up from Broadway so we turned left across a field after the Snowshill crossroads then, as we ascended a path at the edge of more woodland we stopped for a morning break in the sun, sheltered from the cold breeze. I ate an apple. After reaching the top we continued along the ridge to Broadway Tower, not pausing for long on the exposed hilltop there, then taking a photo of sheep near a gate. We stopped for lunch at a picnic site but by then the sun had left us, unfortunately. We refuelled at a picnic table then moved on, crossing an open field on a rough, stony, uneven path. This was the coldest part of the day in that chilly breeze, but not for long; a few fields later we reached the lane into Chipping Campden and found some tearooms with a welcome pot of tea and a scone, first having bought postcards and visited a baker's. There were too many cars about to take a pleasing photo of the lovely stone buildings - cars were a problem for spoiling a possible photo in other places too - so we left on a field path and took photos looking back from the fields to the village then we continued by field and lane to Ebrington, arriving at 5 o'clock at Dave Peachey's Uncle Cyril's farm.

We pitched our tents in the field behind the farm and made hot drinks then went to the pub nearby at 7pm, only a few minutes' walk. What we thought were main courses at £5.40 were starters! Nevertheless, I had the smoked haddock mornay, served with thick slices of bread and butter, but it would have been nice to have had some vegetables with it. They wouldn't even let me pay extra for some vegetables. Dave said the pub had changed hands, previously having served more reasonable meals. Anne was less satisfied with her salad "starter." I dried my socks by the fire before we returned to the tents and settled in as the clock struck ten. I think Dave said we walked 14 miles today. I heard the clock strike 2, also 5, and then 7 - time to get up! I did sleep well between these times.

Wednesday 10th March
- Ebrington to Bidford-on-Avon:

It was not as cold as expected last night but I wore thick socks just in case. As we packed there was the bitter wind again, so I put on warm mitts. I asked if I could buy a couple of eggs but Dave's uncle gave me two new laid ones. Lovely. We'd given him £2.50 each for camping. Now we walked on up the track from the farm, with some shelter from the wind and soon warmed up. We heard our first skylark too, singing above us. Wood pigeons were busy cooing early this morning. The only flowers I remember were coltsfoot, apart from daffodils. We descended to Hidcote (NT); the gardens were not open until the end of the month, nor the other gardens nearby at Kiftsgate Court. We sat in a field below a wall here, warm and sheltered, a sweep of grass leading to woodland opposite and below us. As we walked down the slope I took a photo of the others walking on then I caught up with them at the bottom where more fields and woodland took us to Mickleton. The lambs in these fields were well grown, perhaps 3 or 4 weeks old. Mickleton had an attractive church, but we could see no name other than something like "Cotswold Group of Churches," and stone cottages and a useful village shop where I bought a banana and Dave P and I shared a packet of four Hot Cross buns.

The path crossed more fields with a view of Meon Hill, which seemed to be the final hill of the Cotswolds at 194 metres; the map showed infrequent contours on the route ahead of us. I took a photo of the hill as we approached. The Way passed through Upper and Lower Quinton. Soon after this (12.45pm) Anne and I became hungry but the men wanted to go on to an old railway/cycleway for lunch, so by twenty past one when we stopped Anne and I were *very* hungry. Dave B went on to a pub while Dave P and Anne sat on a wooden bench and I sat behind it out of the wind, in comfort on my sit mat with legs stretched out on the folded flysheet, boots and socks off. When we'd eaten we proceeded to the Mason's Arms, where Dave Bennett had gone, for a welcome pot of tea - we were the only ones in there. The landlady said she wouldn't have a dog because it wouldn't be fair for it to be shut in the flat all day, or if allowed to wander and make friends with the customers it would be a friend to all and not guard against intruders.

The path now went behind some black and white cottages and across fields then eventually came to what were shown as orchards on my 20 year old map, but they are just fields now, then a track soon led into Barton, near Bidford-on-Avon, with the Cottage of Comfort (pub/campsite) in sight. Nobody was about so we pitched at the far end of the field, for peace and quiet, then Dave Peachey and I accompanied Anne along the riverside path to Bidford-on-Avon where she had to get a bus in order to be home for a commitment the following day. It was nice to see Anne off on her bus then we had a brisk walk back across the fields to the campsite, where I cooked a meal, made use of the phone outside, then went into the pub where the Daves were already eating...they told me they'd paid my pitch fees for me - £6.50! Isn't that shocking! - not even including a shower, just a tiny basin in the toilets, and just for one person! I thought the landlady could afford to sponsor me after that so I asked her if she'd like to sign my form and give a donation. She did.

Thursday 11th March
- Bidford-on-Avon via Alcester to Henley-in-Arden:

We all set off at 8.30, the Daves making for Stratford, and I made good time through Bidford and on by paths and lane to Wixford, where a short path across a field of horses led me to the Roman Road which becomes a bridleway. When I found a spot sheltered from the wind, which was after four miles, I had a break with boots off the write yesterday's diary, which I had not done last night due to spending the evening in the pub with the others. The bridleway led between trees then descended to a roundabout - this wasn't on the map; a new road was here - but the bridleway was indicated on the other side and took me to a lane then footpath to Alcester. I liked Alcester. Here I saw a bakery so I went in for rolls, one filled with chicken & salad and one plain wholemeal, then there was a greengrocer where I bought a large pear, the large one being the only one ripe enough to eat, and a pint of milk. The street of small, varied shops took me to St Nicholas Church, where the road curved round. There was a handy seat here, which turned out to have been given to Alcester by the Heart of England Way Association, so I decided to sit there to eat the (8oz?) pear then I took a photo of the church, including the seat.

Now I continued along the road until a footpath on the left led through some trees and over open, dry fields, the first field actually having a trig pillar, where I took a photo. Way finding was mostly easy but in one place an arrow pointed straight on, so straight on I went, to find no stile or gate all along the hedge so I returned to the stile, got out the compass to find that the path should go slightly to the left to the other hedge and lane, where there was stile hidden behind a trailer. The next path again went through green fields passing a small hill called Round Hill. Later a bridleway was followed by a permissive path through and round Bannam's Wood, not quite as the map showed the right of way, but pleasant walking.

Across a lane the path continued and after the first field I stopped beyond the hedge for shelter to have a drink of water. At that point a man appeared, a day walker, and stopped to chat about what I was doing and the Cotswold Way, which he planned to do. He offered me some orange squash, as he'd got far more than he wanted. I then proceeded to Henley-in-Arden, along a path that was not too clear in places, then passing between allotments and over the railway footbridge at the station before what seemed a long detour into the attractive little town.

The way out was past the church then a path climbed the hill then undulated gently over more level tops across dry fields. I had drunk the last of my water/orange squash and was thinking of a pitch for the night. Now, the best thing would be to ask at a farm or farms on the way to Lowsonford, in case the pub (The Fleur de Lys) there says No. The first habitation was a lovely old house with stables so, if stables, there was possibly a field. I went the short distance up the track and rang the bell. A pleasant lady answered the door and when I asked about a sheltered spot for a small tent she said, "Oh, you must be cold - you can go on the lawn next to the house. Do come in and have a cup of tea, and have something to eat with us!" I said I'd be pitched in about ten minutes, and after a cup of tea, I had a luxurious shower and hairwash, then a sit and chat with Sonia's friend, Maureen, before dinner at seven, which was cottage pie, sausages, mash, carrots, broccoli, cabbage, wine, banana and ice cream. All delicious. Sonia and Greg's son, Ross, and daughter, Alexis - horse owner and keen eventer - as well as Maureen and I enjoyed the meal. It turned out that both Sonia and Maureen used to work for Barclays Bank, as I did years ago, and Maureen had broken an arm and a leg last year, and was in hospital when I was, although unfortunately with a broken arm she could not use crutches. That must have been very frustrating.

Then we went sat and talked until about ten to ten, when I was given a hot water bottle to return to the tent. That was luxury indeed, but I must remember to remove it before it gets cold.

It was a lovely evening, one to remember, with lovely people.

Friday 12th March 2004
- Henley-in-Arden to Meriden, Queen's Head:

I slept well, the hot water bottle having warmed my nightwear of Tracksters and Damart top and then my feet. It was peaceful here - all I heard when I woke in the night was the whisper of snow (which had been forecast) on the flysheet. In the morning I gave the flysheet a kick and a thump to send the snow sliding down. I had been told that the door would be left unlocked so that I could use the downstairs cloakroom, and that breakfast would be about 8 o'clock. I packed all except the flysheet before going in for a wash, then I sat at the kitchen table, welcomed by the dogs, to write my diary until Sonia appeared. Breakfast was cereal, toast and marmalade and tea, but of course we were talking so I left at 9.50 instead of 9am. Never mind. First I took a couple of photos of the tent in the snow before I packed the flysheet and went in to warm my hands and gloves, and say thank you and goodbye to these kind and generous people.

I turned down the snowy track to snowy fields, seeing tracks of birds, rabbit and hare. I observed the Fleur de Lys at Lowsonford, noting that there was a large beer garden in case I'd ended up pitching there, then went on to the canal bank, up to Kings Lapworth, where a man behind the pub said the path I was looking for was a dead end, so I returned to the canal for another mile then went along the lane past Baddesley Clinton and on over more snowy fields. Baddesley Clinton (National Trust) would be open at 12 o'clock for "Daffodil Walks" but I could not wait until then, having some way to go to Meriden.

Reading the footprints, I could see that a man and a dog had walked one path; four people had walked another path and only my footprints were visible on others. At Chadwick End the PO was closed (on Wednesdays and Fridays).

In TGO it was reported that a footpath on the Heart of England way had been closed near Balsall Common due to badger activity, which was bit worrying. However, a notice on a stile told of a diversion and a footpath and lane made very little difference to the distance walked. I stopped on a stile for my lunch - warmer than sitting in the snow! Easy field paths led past Balsall Common; I could look back and see my footprints in the snow stretching across two fields and the footbridge between. A lane led to a surprisingly quiet crossing of the A452 Kenilworth road then from the lane a woodland path then parkland took me to Berkswell Church. I sat in a field corner to cool my feet, have a snack and drink of water before the final 2½ miles to Meriden. I had just pitched behind the Queen's Head, after clearing a circle of snow, and fetched some water, when Tony Wilson appeared - a nice surprise. He was joining me for Saturday's walk and half of Sunday's route. We spent the evening in the pub, where again we were not charged for camping due to doing the walk for charity, and caught up with Backpackers Club news and Tony's photos.

Saturday 13th March
- Meriden to Kingsbury Water Park:

We left at nine o'clock, first visiting Meriden, where I wanted to buy cheese, rolls and fruit, then we looked at and took photos of the 500 year old cross marking the centre of England. A man on the road leading out of town explained the new road and path layout for crossing the A45, then we got back on our planned route - Tony had the adjoining map, Landranger140, so we could use footpaths instead of the "yellow roads" that I'd intended to use, not having sheet 140, and returned to the Heart of England Way. I had not thought it worth buying sheet 140 because there was only a very short section of the walk on it.

Some of these fields were sticky after the melted snow and made heavy going and muddy boots. We saw buzzards and heard skylarks and saw the first celandines. Our lunch stop was at The Griffin, Church End, Shustoke, monthly meeting place of the West Midlands Backpackers, while a convenient shower rattled on the conservatory where we were sitting. I picked up two sprouts out-side! Now footpaths led to and past Shustoke Reservoir but there were few views of the water due to trees growing between it and the path. We soon crossed the railway to another path to Hoggrill's End then lanes through Whiteacre Heath to Lea Marston where a bridleway took us on soft woodchips - now on the Centenary Way - past pools of water. We sat down on the soft woodchips for a break here, passed by ponies and dog walkers, then on we went for the last leg. After crossing the A4097 a narrow road at Bodymoor Heath led us through woods and by waterside to Kingsbury Water Park. We stopped to take a photo of Kingsbury Church across the River Tame, then past the pools with the odd swan and several Canada geese, we came to the Kingsbury Water Park Campsite.

We were made welcome; I was given my food parcel and we were advised that over by the hedge would be sheltered from the wind. Kind people from a nearby caravan brought us mugs of tea while we were pitching, then I put food to soak and went for a luxurious shower in the warm shower block. Lovely. I'm sure there was underfloor heating - it was so warm to step out on to the red tiles from the shower. I unpacked the food parcel and read a note from Sandra and Brian. They had even put in a piece of Sandra's homemade fruit cake and three apples and some nuts and raisins and some more muesli and had replaced the shortbread that I had told them to eat last year. I'll have to do some eating to reduce the weight! At about 8 o'clock Tony and I went to the pub, the Dog & Doublet, when we found it in the dark, although it was not far away. The landlord gave a donation for the walk, as did the couple at the next table. Tony noticed that I was nodding off - so I was, and slept well back at the tent in spite of traffic not far away. It was another good day.

Sunday 14th March
- Kingsbury Water Park via Lichfield to Chorley:

This is an excellent campsite with marvellous washing facilities, and at £4 per person it is certainly good value, although we didn't have to pay, again due to my doing it for charity and Tony accompanying me even though it was only for a weekend. We set off at ten to nine and were soon on the canal bank. Tony suggested a path on the other side of the canal at the second bridge, passing jungle-like between Canary reeds then through a field to the left and thence to a pond with trees and an island, then we continued along a lane and road to a Craft Centre. I said I thought that pots of tea were likely there but Tony was doubtful, but then I have probably visited more craft centres than Tony has! However, it was open and there *was* a tearoom, where we had a pot of tea for two and toasted teacakes, then had the pot topped up. This was well timed as a shower of rain rattled on the window, but it was still raining when we emerged so we put on overtrousers.

A bit of road walking took us to the lane leading to the farms shown on the map, but these were now housing. At Rookery Farm Tony took a photo of me at the signpost showing the Heart of England Way sign, then we had our lunch on a grassy bank a bit further on. Here we said Goodbye, for Tony was making his way to Tamworth for a train home and I was obviously heading onward along the Heart of England Way.

It was pleasant, easy walking, over a hill and down a dip and up past a field of horses to the road, then past the next farm up a track where I was ready to sit down for an apple while I aired my feet, sitting behind a farm roller. Soon after this I encountered an awkward-to-climb hurdle (instead of a stile or gate) then a bridleway led to and across a road and proceeded dead straight - perhaps it had been a Roman road? - for some way and it made good walking all the way to edge of Lichfield.

The tiring bit was the road walking into Lichfield with nowhere to sit down and a hard surface underfoot, but my spirits lifted as I drew closer to the cathedral towers and I eventually sat down on a seat outside the west end for a few minutes. (I did not go in because I was concerned about finding a pitch for the night, and had been inside the cathedral before, several years ago).

Just before the cathedral, on a corner, was a circular metal plaque set into a paving slab: "Heart of England Way" and two arrows, which was interesting and worth a photo. There was some way to go before I could hope to pitch so I set off again, along Cathedral Close then a road and a footpath at the outer edge of a park until it reached the A38. From here I used the lane instead of the Heart of England Way path, so that I'd be where any farms were, but I actually walked three miles from the cathedral (total 17 for the day) to the village of Chorley and Chorley Close Farm. Even Chorley Close Farm, shown on the map, had been converted to houses: Farmhouse Cottage, Stables House etc. There was no reply at the former when I rang the bell but the people at Stables House kindly let me camp, if I didn't mind the ponies in the field, which of course I did not, and there was a tap at the gate. Then the people from Farmhouse Cottage came and asked if I'd like to come in for a cup of tea and a shower, which were very welcome - shower first then mug of tea and a chat with them. He came from Scotland and was a keen fisherman. In the end it was eight o'clock when I cooked my meal and I was tired by the time I had washed up at nine o'clock so I soon settled down for sleep. Except for the road walk into Lichfield, it has been an enjoyable day.

Monday 15th March
- Chorley via Cannock Chase to Little Haywood:

The morning started bright and sunny with birds singing. Again I was offered use of facilities in the house, this time downstairs as the bathroom was occupied. At 7 o'clock I finished my film on tent and ponies and changed it. The girls came to feed their ponies and said their Mum said would I like tea and toast, which was very kind, but I'd had most of my breakfast by then and caught up on some diary writing so didn't leave until half past nine.

As I walked past, I noted that The Malt Shovel had a grassy beer garden, in case anyone should think of asking to camp there, then I posted off some maps and a film before continuing mostly along narrow lanes towards Cannock Chase. It seemed to take a long time to get there, with just one footpath to break up the road walking. At last a diverted path led on to Cannock Chase near the Castle Ring embankment, which is all there is to see, then woodland tracks lead on. I had not been on this southern part of the Chase before, only north from the Boulder Stone. At grid ref. 000159 I left the map, Landranger 128, having just sat down out of the wind on a bank for lunch. Not having sheet 127, I had removed a page from the old Staffordshire Way booklet to use instead and used the compass in conjunction with the Heart of England way signs.

I saw the odd cyclist and dog walkers and enjoyed the open stretches with views over wooded hills, and the paths between the trees, but the stony tracks were not comfortable underfoot. I stopped for a snack and drink of water at some birch trees in an area of open heather, some time after the Polish Katyn War Memorial. Then I saw a signpost not far away and got out the binoculars to read "STAFFS WAY" - that was an exciting step forward and called for a photo with the rucksack at the base of the signpost. A man walking that way said that it obviously meant something to me so would I like a photo with me on? Soon after this an arrow pointed down to the right for Sherbrook Valley, which is lovely with its clear stream, remembered from walking the Staffordshire Way about twenty years ago. At the Stepping Stones I decided to cross and head for Seven Springs, as I had not been there before, taking a photo of the stepping stones first.

From Seven Springs a lane leads from the car park, crosses a road and bridge then under two railway bridges with the canal between, to reach Little Haywood. It was half a mile up to Park

View Farm, where I thought I'd enquire about camping, although it was early, but they said No, they were closed and had sheep in the field (I didn't see any sheep but it didn't matter). So, I returned to the canal (Staffordshire Way) and asked at some cottages along the towpath. From the end one I obtained water - he said his dog would bark all night if he let me camp in the garden - and I carried it along the canal bank for a short way until the grass widens just before the railway, as the man at the cottage had told me it would. Frequent trains passing did not bother me as they rattled over the bridge. I was soon pitched and tucking into mug of tea, pan of mixed beans, varied pasta twists, vegetables and garlic sauce followed by banana custard. After washing up I phoned Anne to update her on my progress. Now I am yawning so will have an early night. I think it was only about 12-13 miles today, but it was a lovely Cannock Chase day, and a step forward on to the Staffordshire Way! Now I can hear the patter of raindrops.

Tuesday 16th March 2004
- Little Haywood to the former Eatonhall Farm near Rocester:
The last train clattered over the bridge at 10.30 last night and there was not another until after six o'clock this morning, which was not at all disturbing. I also heard the birds: robin, wren, blue tit, wood pigeon and moorhen, but mostly the wren in the hawthorn hedge, where the buds are just bursting. I had porridge, baked beans and oatcakes for breakfast and, after an early night, I had an early start. It seems strange that this is the Trent and Mersey Canal, my home canal. If I had chosen that route it would probably only have taken two days to walk home along the towpath, but I had other plans. As it was a fair distance to my hoped for pitch at Eaton Hall Farm, between Uttoxeter and Rocester, I started at 8.32am, walking between the canal and the river, with a thrush singing and celandines and coltsfoot adding colour, and later the first pink flowers of butterbur. Canada geese flew over and I saw an oystercatcher, after hearing it first, by the river.

The 2½ miles of canal were soon past then a track left the canal for the road, and a field path with the blue of speedwell here and there led to Colton, then lanes and paths took me to Colwich and Abbott's Bromley.

As I remembered, not much of Blithfield Reservoir can be seen due to the path taking you down below the dam and looping away from it, so you can only see the water before reaching and after leaving the area of lower land by the dam. There were pleasant paths to Abbott's Bromley entering the village through the church-yard. I went first to the Post Office then to the shop near the pub for a postcard then into The Crown for some excellent Broccoli and Stilton soup with roll and butter. They donated £5 and told me that I could get eggs at the butchers down the road. I also bought an apple, tomato and cheese there before collecting my rucksack from outside the pub then proceeding up Schoolhouse Lane, round the corner, and on to the open spaces of Bagot's Park.

Waymarks direct one around fields, not quite following the right of way shown on the map. After an hour's walking I sat down in a field to air my feet and eat the large apple to save weight. It was warm and sunny now so I was down to T-shirt and windshirt. The miles soon passed but I did not see the spot where, in 1984, I remember rescuing the lamb with its head caught in the wire mesh fence with a tap dripping on its neck; it was mostly crops in the fields here now and some grassland with no livestock about. Perhaps that fence is no longer there.

There were awkward stiles after Marl Pit Farm, then almost a direct line to Uttoxeter, where a new road at the bottom of Balance Hill had to be crossed then I made my way with map and compass, by now with slightly sore feet, towards Dove Bridge, the latter part being along a walk/cycle way with the path leading under the new bridge (spoiling the view of the old bridge) to reach the field path out to Eatonhall Farm....I was surprised here by a sign announcing that it was a clay pigeon shooting place now. I'd heard long-tailed tits and seen about six of them in the hedge just before I arrived, almost at sunset.

Fortunately I was allowed to camp and have use of water and toilet at the Clubhouse, the large building I'd just passed. In ten minutes the tent was pitched; I washed and fetched water and soon settled in for a meal, hearing snipe and pheasant nearby, but before cooking I popped out to take a photo of the last of the sunset.

Today was a satisfying day of 17½ miles.

Wednesday 17th March 2004
- Eatonhall Farm, near Rocester to just before Kingsley Holt, via Alton:

The noise of the traffic on the A50 could be heard here, over a mile away, but only in the background so I slept well. The nearer sounds were provided by birds calling and singing. After porridge, scrambled egg and toast I washed up then wrote yesterday's diary between eight and half past. I started walking at ten past nine on a cloudy morning. It was rather sad to see that the old farm buildings of Eatonhall Farm were being demolished. I had written on my map "Lee & Michelle 1984" beside the farm, after Paula and I had camped there that year, when the old farmhouse and buildings looked very attractive and in good repair. The next farm, Eaton Dovedale, looked in better condition but at the next one, Sedsall, I think, (there's a worn fold in the old map), the house was boarded up with a danger sign displayed and the land was unused. By Abbotsholme School playing fields there were Millennium Path signs following the bank of the River Dove so I followed them, which made the route slightly further but pleasant riverside walking. I heard the first chiffchaff of this spring calling from bushes in the last field before the road.

Rocester was not as attractive as Abbott's Bromley. The Londis shop was all right for a banana, milk and chocolate but large oranges were packed in twenties and apples in fours - no good to a backpacker - and the assistant was having a long conversation with the customer before me so I wanted to get out quickly. A new road or road junction was a puzzle at first with no signs to the path by the bridge, which took a while to find. I followed it uphill to a wood, where I stopped to eat the banana before entering the wood over a stile. Here I saw my first wood anemones of the spring, just beginning to flower by a plank footbridge - rather rotten planks! There were the leaves of bluebells, violets and dog's mercury and beyond the wood were a few primroses. There was no waymark at a new gate but the binoculars enabled me to see across the field to a stile with a yellow arrow. This turned out to be two stiles with a ditch between - a plank or two would help here.

Next I came to a lovely stone bridge at Quixall, where I took a photo before reaching the road and continuing to the next field path on the Staffordshire Way, then a paved way led for some distance to a farm then a stile on the right gave access to a path across the fields to Alton. There had been nowhere scenic or mud-free to sit down for lunch so I continued through Alton down to the River Churnet and lunch by the side of the lane overlooking the river. (Cheese roll and fruit cake). Soon after this what did I come across? The Ramblers Retreat, where I'd been twenty years ago with Paula on the Staffordshire Way, and we'd enjoyed toasted teacakes and shelter from the rain. I had to go in, if "in" is the word for having a pot of tea and scone outside in the garden watching bluetits and great tits at the bird feeders, and a robin landed on my table. There was also a crow near a small waterfall in the wood above the garden, apparently trying to find something to eat in the water.

Now time was getting on so I proceeded up the woodland walk then through Hawksmoor Nature Reserve to East Walls Farm (National Trust), then across a field full of sheep and lambs and a cow with two calves. Two or three fields later a stile led to a stream then some rough set-aside land before the next grazed field. I wondered (perhaps aloud), "What about this corner by the river under the trees?" I could go back for water - the stream in the next field was muddy, trampled by cattle - I went back, leaving the rucksack under a tree, then returned to hang the water bag from the tree because it leaked when lying flat. The ground is a bit tussocky and I removed several twigs but it is comfortable enough. I enjoyed a meal, washed up, washed self and clothes then listened to Classic FM and to the River Churnet below me. Now for some Horlicks and an early night. Before I settled down I saw headlights shining towards the tent and thought, "How can that be - there's no road!" Then I realised that the lights came from across the river, and possibly the farmer on the other side had seen the light of my headtorch and thought that someone was fishing here. The tractor or Landrover turned away and the lights vanished.

Today was only 11½ miles but a most enjoyable, unrushed and scenic spring day.

Thursday 18th March
- Kingsley Holt via Rudyard Lake to Rushton Spencer:
Rain pattered on the tent in the night, and again this morning I could hear rain, and the River Churnet rushing over rocks below me and a thrush singing above me. I set off at five to nine, crossed the stile into the next field, and the stream in its deep muddy channel and across to Kingsley Holt and on to Kingsley, where there

was a phone box so I phoned Dad. From the phone the Staffordshire Way took some finding, but I did eventually and crossed two or three fields to the woodland with the close contours. My presence was announced by geese. Fortunately there were steps down through the steep woodland as far as the lane, which made it easier. Bluebell leaves promised a sea of blue later on. Across the lane a grassy path descended through old, dead bracken and birches then ahead was the River Churnet again and the Cheddleton Railway Bridge over it.

From here the path went up to the towpath of the Caldon canal, where I stopped for a snack beside a solitary daffodil. It was still misty here but no longer raining. After twenty minutes I strode on again, fuelled by the water and the nuts and raisins that Brian and Sandra had added to my food parcel. The miles along the canal passed quickly, punctuated by one or two pauses for photos. At exactly one o'clock I reached a grassy patch above Cheddleton Flint Mill, after 8½ miles, and removed boots and socks to stretch out my legs on the polythene sheet while I had my oatcakes with garlic and herb pate. At 1.40pm I was off again, seeing butterbur by the canal and mallards and Canada geese on it, then I heard the "Veni, Vidi, Vici" bird, so it is not only found in the Cotswolds and Warwickshire woodlands. This was high up in a tree - I actually saw it, but in silhouette as the sun was behind the tree so I couldn't see the colours and still can't identify it. The sun only shone for a brief spell.

Near Denford the Staffordshire Way leaves the canal to make for Ladderedge Country Park, heading up along a bridleway to cross the road and winds down to the park. Soon after this there was a view of the Roaches so I took a photo, then as I emerged from the trees and walked down to the canal feeder, rain started, serious rain. I sat on my rucksack under a tree for a while to shelter and to rest my aching left foot or heel, which felt better when I moved on again. Suddenly the rain stopped and ahead of me was clear blue sky and bright green fields. Lovely. There was even a seat by the path so I had a short sit down and took a photo. I moved forward steadily, not fast because of the mud after the rain, but I made good time to Rudyard although I was ready to sit down when I got there. I drank the rest of my water and had some shortbread and chocolate sitting under a tree, then I got to my feet for the final miles along Rudyard Lake, again at a steady pace.

There was The Cloud ahead - another landmark and another photo, where the trees opened out to give a better view. I'd walked all that way to see The Cloud - the hill that is only about 13 miles from home! My feet were a bit sore under the toes now (getting used to the Sorbothane heel pads, which put more weight on to the toes, I think) so I chose the softest parts of the old railway track to walk on. From five minutes to five at Rudyard I reached Rushton at six o'clock, so that was quite good, and went into the pub to enquire about camping - they had a large beer garden. No, I couldn't use the beer garden because the pub belonged to the brewery but I could have some water and take it back along the old railway past the car park to the area with a picnic table and hedge shelter; I had seen that corner by the picnic table as I had passed. I pitched quickly, removed muddy boots and overtrousers, took water bottles to the pub and had a glass of grapefruit juice with ice in. Two people gave donations for the Walk then I had a wash before returning to cook a meal. I enjoyed the warmth and brightness of two nightlights until the old one was finished, then I washed up and washed my feet, then phoned Anne Ling and Stella. I'm looking forward to walking with Stella, Barbara and Katie tomorrow. Now I'm ready to settle down after 18 miles today.

It has been a good day in spite of mist and rain.

Friday 19th March
- Rushton to Macclesfield:

Rain pattered down on the tent at ten past six this morning but a wren was singing cheerfully. I had slept well. The forecast wind rushed through the trees but didn't reach the tent in its sheltered corner. After breakfast I looked at the map. Congleton caught my eye first, surprising me after so many maps full of unknown or lesser-known names. I think I shall use mostly lanes to the Macclesfield Canal to avoid mud in the fields. It is now twenty past eight; the rain is still pelting down and I shall finish packing now.

It had actually stopped raining when I started walking and further along the old railway track the sun was shining. The path left the railway to cross a field and go up through lovely woodland - I'd forgotten it was there; it must be years ago that I walked that section of the Staffordshire Way. That's another place that will have bluebells later on. I used some of the Dane Valley Way for my route to the canal and found it less muddy than I had expected, even the large field just before the canal that had been muddy in December 2001 on the Dane Valley Way walk. I had a short break in the woodland just before the canal, where it was sheltered from the wind, then joined the canal towpath to walk briskly and made good time - I had to watch the time as I was meeting Stella, Barbara and Katie at Fool's Nook at 12.30pm.

Anyway, I timed it well and arrived first, but only because they had driven too far and had to turn back to the pub. I changed out of my boots by the wall in the car park while I was waiting, then we all went in and enjoyed jacket potatoes with various fillings, and catching up with each other's news, then after I'd taken a photo of them outside, we all walked on along the canal, intending to walk along the towpath to Macclesfield. However, near Gurnet there was a barrier across the towpath with a notice saying that it was closed, but closed for how far would it be, before we could rejoin it? We didn't know, but went down to the road near the King's Head and walked on along roads and streets into Macclesfield, trying here and there to find access to the towpath again, each time finding it closed. That was disappointing for the others who had been expecting a nice towpath walk, and they had to return that way to go back to their car at Fool's Nook. It was nice to have the pleasure of their company.

My arrangement here was to stay at Pat & Steve's overnight at Tytherington, so I phoned Pat to arrange where to meet her. This was at a car park at the Ranger station she said, where the Bollin Way is a convenient dog walk for them. She would be walking Tess and their new pup, Ted. I think I arrived about ten minutes before Pat and the dogs - lovely to meet Ted with his soft brown velvety coat - Pat said his mother was called Velvet. We walked back to their house and had a lovely meal when Steve came home from work and caught up with their news during the evening.

Next morning, Saturday, I took a photo of Pat and Steve and the dogs outside their conservatory before leaving to catch the bus home. (I had to be home for my final hospital visit next week). While in Macclesfield, before catching the 10am bus, I bought a new mobile phone battery. I think this will solve the problem of re-charging the battery; I can fully charge the two batteries and make them last about a fortnight each. I had hoped to use my solar charger but the sun did not shine when needed, or did not shine for long enough, and a small wind-up charger only gives an emergency charge not a full one.

My final hospital appointment is on Tuesday but I am sure that all is well; my left leg feels as good as my right leg and hasn't given any problems. I'm looking forward to getting a bus back to Macclesfield on Thursday to continue northward once more.

Thursday 25th March
- Macclesfield to High Lane near Hazel Grove via canal and Middlewood Way:

The first part of this morning was spent doing the odd jobs that I was too tired to do last night, such as lunches of rolls and cheese, bagging some dehydrated baked beans and slicing the fruit cake made yesterday, then it was time to go for the bus. Light rain made overtrousers a good idea, although the rain had stopped by the time I reached the bus stop.

The bus driver said, "You should be walking, not getting a bus!" I replied that I'd left Macclesfield on Saturday and was returning to continue my Land's End to John O'Groats walk. The bus arrived at Macclesfield at about five to twelve; I sat down to put my boots on, then headed past the station and up the Buxton road, hoping for canal access this time. I was lucky - it was here that the closed section of the towpath ended so I went down the steps and along a slightly muddy towpath. There were a fair number of joggers and dog walkers about. I continued to Bollington, past Whitely Green, where we met for Pat & Steve's Cheshire Backpackers meal last June, and here I joined the Middlewood Way for a change of scene. It is divided in two, part for walkers and cyclists and part for horses. Blackthorn blossomed and a robin sang; Alderley Edge was visible. I sat down when there was a picnic table or seat, seeing chaffinches and blue tits, then on again and made good time on this level walking.

The last part before I left it for High Lane was very muddy in the walkers' half - I should have changed to the horses' side - so my lovely clean boots were clean no more. I came up to the road, observed a phone box a few minutes' walk down it, then phoned Lesley. She and Lawrence picked me up a few minutes later, after I'd crossed to the other side of the road. It turned out to be Lawrence's birthday so we had a cup of tea and slice of good, rich fruit birthday cake when I arrived, then later a delicious meal of soup, roast pork etc. After washing up we looked at their photos of various Back-packers Club weekends including the snowy Old/New Year break in Snowdonia, so it was delightful evening altogether.

Although the distance was only 8 or 8½ miles today it was still northward progress and most of the Middlewood Way is new to me - I had only walked a short section at Bollington years ago. I had changed my old, worn footbeds while at home and replaced them with a pair from another pair of boots, which felt much better underfoot. Along the canal bank the flowers were butterbur, celandines and coltsfoot.

Friday 26th March
- High Lane to Greenside near Werneth Low:

I slept well last night, and later than I expected, which was prob-ably due to staying up late doing things on Wednesday night. I had breakfast with Lesley, Lawrence having gone to work while I was sound asleep. She kindly packed up some lunch for me, including a piece of Lawrence's delicious birthday cake, then took me back to the Middlewood Way at High Lane where I'd left it yesterday after-noon. Lesley took a photo of me at the Middlewood Way informa-tion board before saying Goodbye.

Soon I was striding away along the path, which was better drained than yesterday's muddy bit. After a mile and a half, sooner than I expected, I saw a sign on the right and a stile for a footpath that crosses a golf course, after a woodland walk to a stream, and dodged the golfers as the path led across to the canal towpath at Marple. A roving bridge took me to the other bank then, after a short distance I could see the other roving bridge ahead, remem-bered from foot and mouth year. I took a photo although I already had a print. This bridge is on the postcard that I sent to Jim & Maggie. I just went up, across the road and along where a sign pointed along the Goyt Way...but I didn't look at the map until the first bridge; when I looked the compass needle pointed south - the wrong way! The map said the other way, where the towpath went down a series of locks and through an interesting little key-hole-type tunnel under the road. The next bit of towpath was above the woodland of Brabyns Park.

The map did not show clearly just where one got down on to the Goyt Way below but a lady with a dog suddenly vanished through a gap in the wall where steps led to a woodland path with a Goyt

Way sign at the bottom. The path curved round by the river and continued towards Compstall over an old iron bridge that was being restored. At the Post Office at Compstall I bought a pint of milk asked if they sold postcards. Yes, but until I'd paid for it they didn't tell me how much it was. 95p for milk and card sounded a lot - the card was 50p! Anyway, when I stopped up the hill past Beacon Houses I wrote the card to Jean and Arthur.

The plan was to turn right at the top of the hill, down to Idle Hill, then down to the A560 as a possible "connect up point" for a bus tomorrow (but Will, who has the next food parcel, says that buses don't go that way from Woodley) then from Greenside head down to the next path up Werneth Low. This path climbed steeply to the War Memorial with cloudy views to Bleaklow and Black Hill, then south to cross the lane, then I turned right on a path to rejoin the lane, past the pub on a bridleway, then down to Woodley. To Will's Mill this made a total of 11 miles. After a nice meal with Will I sorted out the food parcel - the contents will obviously add to my weight tomorrow but I have had two easy days. It will be good to get up into the hills again.

Today's walking has been varied, just lacking the views due to cloud and a bit of drizzle, but there have been "many options," as Tony Wilson would say, in the choice of route.

Saturday 27th March
- Greenside to above Dovestone Reservoir, near Greenfield:

There was no bus, as Will had said, to take us from Woodley to my "connecting up point" at Greenside, but a bus did save us at least ½ mile of road walking to get back on the route, then we "connected up" and walked on past Little Acre Stables and Greenside Cattery to the wood near the railway. A slightly muddy path wound between the trees, where it was very pleasant but there were no spring flowers to be seen yet. Later we came to the former Hodge Field Bleach and Dye Works with old stone tanks in the valley, quite a group of them, dating from 1805, nearly 200 years ago. The track went into a lane passing some weavers' cottages with their long upper storey windows, then we passed under a railway bridge, steeply uphill, through Broadbottom and uphill again to a footpath across the fields, later giving views up Longdendale and back to Mottram Church on its hill. Young Jersey cattle including a bull looked at us from a farm building, but the farmer said he wasn't allowed to sell untreated milk.

Across the main road the Coach Road, mostly bridleway, led to Mottram Old Hall, where a path left it to cross a field occupied by three horses. We were hungry by now so decided, horses permitting, that we'd stop for lunch on a bank by the trees half way up the field. The bay horse investigated first, then the chestnut but the dark bay was more aloof. The bay nuzzled my rucksack frequently, possibly smelling the apple inside, but we were able to eat our lunch without requests for food, only friendly nuzzles and blowing down nostrils, which was quite pleasant actually, for me. When we moved they accompanied us up the field with a final kick up of the heels and a canter as we made our way to the stile. The lane or track passed two farms then to another lane to Hollingworth Hall, past which we had views of open country and wild Pennines.

We had a break on a broken wall while sheep grazed nearby, curlews and lapwings called and meadow pipits chirped. This was easy walking, gently undulating, and then eventually a stile led to the permissive path leading to Chew Reservoir. Last time we had walked in mist and rain from the stile and used a compass bearing for the Reservoir - this time we could see to follow the "path" through a not too boggy area to the edge, where the path was better, rockier, and made easy walking. As we neared Chew we cut down to cross the stream and climb up the other side, across the reservoir track and on up to the path round the edge above the Greenfield reservoirs. This path is not shown on the map but I had walked it before (train to Greenfield for a day walk). We followed the edge round above Dovestone Reservoir and found a pitch on tussocks of comfortable mat grass with a bit of heather and bilberry, only about 25 yards from the waterfall. This has been an interesting and satisfying day's walk.

Sunday 28th March 2004
- Dovestone Edge to Aiggin Stone, after Blackstone Edge:

We did remember to put our watches on an hour last night and woke about seven o'clock. Breakfast was porridge and boiled egg. I wrote some diary, being too tired last night after traffic had kept me awake the night before, then we set off about 9.10 or 9.15, I think, following the path on round the edge. From the waterfall it is a right of way leading to a stile but after this it peters out. There were two lambs on the hillside with the ewe not far away. We descended steeply, with me sitting down to slide down, to the stream, which we crossed on stones, and went round the other side of the spur to follow the next stream/ravine until it was possible to descend and cross it. This left about half a mile of rough country, bog and heather, to cross going due north to the road (A635, Holmfirth) then it was a mile and a half along the road, though mostly there was soft walking at the edge, to where we hoped to find the soup and refreshment caravan at the parking area where the Pennine Way crosses the road. Good! - it *was* there - I asked the man if he was there 20 years ago when I walked the Pennine Way and he said he was, and had he changed? We had oxtail soup and a roll (£1) but it was a breezy spot so we were glad to get moving and crossed the road to continue on the Pennine Way. We sat down in a sheltered corner later on, since we had stood up for lunch for shelter behind the caravan, and I ate my apple here.

It was nice to walk this part of the route without rain. Lower down a man having his lunch recommended crossing the reservoir embankment and continuing round instead of the steep up and down of the Pennine Way. It was longer but probably less strenuous. Now the Pennine Way proper had stretches of flagstones for most of the way as it crossed the moors and between two reservoirs before rising to the next road. We met two ladies going the wrong way because they had no map and were relying on a book of walks. After crossing the road we sat on the bank inside the gate for a drink of water and a snack. Will said he could not go on at my pace (not fast), or at all with his "tight" knees and blisters in new boots (I wonder why he wore new boots?) so he left me at four o'clock. I said I'd go on until seven o'clock and thanked him for his company.

Now I was able to get on at my own pace and strode on over Stand Edge and White Hill at a fair pace to make up for slower early miles but slowed down over Blackstone Edge, picking my way between the rocks and the sun was in my eyes as I came down the other side. It was 7.30pm when I eventually reached the 600-year-old Aiggin Stone. I saw levelish mat grass near it behind the cairn, pitched quickly then had to go some way along the Roman road for water. I soon had a mug of tea, and a meal and washed self and socks. I left a message on Val's answerphone in reply to her text (re

meeting at Ponden) and phoned Tony Wilson to tell him my whereabouts for his website.

I'd say that today's walk was 16 miles, although there was a very
small section of map missing over Stand Edge so it could be 16½
or 17, but certainly 16 at least. The first miles were slow across the
rough open country but the last miles on my own were quick. It was
good to see the sun this afternoon, and wide Pennine views.

Today's birds were: grouse, meadow pipits, and a kestrel, the latter hovering near the road.

Monday 29th March
- The Aiggin Stone via Hebden Bridge to Ponden:

At 6.45 the sky was cloudy-bright and it felt warmer - 45 degrees
now. After muesli, beans, toast and tea I packed and took a photo of
the Aiggin Stone with the tent in the background. A lark sang while
I was packing and more larks sang as I walked. It took an hour
and five minutes to reach Paula's and my old pitch by Lighthazzles
Reservoir, now slightly changed but it was still possible to pitch not
far away. This morning's walking was quick and easy accompanied
by larksong and meadow pipits. Stoodley Pike came into view and
just before it was a lovely clear stream, which was welcome as I had
finished my water. I met a man, then a retired couple walking the
other way, who both asked if I was "doing the whole route" (the
Pennine Way). After a short chat, as I approached the tower I heard
the thin whistling call of a golden plover; there it was, head sticking
up above the rushes.

I did not go up the tower this time but took a photo of the steps
inside before heading down to an awkward step stile over a wall
- the steps on the far side were a bit inadequate so I took off the
rucksack and balanced it and the poles on the wall to get over unladen. The way now went on down the sheep pasture to a signpost -
the Pennine Bridleway. This route would be better for the centre of
Hebden Bridge so I took it then soon stopped in a gateway for my
cheese roll before following lane and path down to Hebden Bridge.
Here the Co-op provided wholemeal teacakes, a tomato, a pint of
milk and Yeo Valley Yoghurt. It took a while to find a shop selling
postcards though. Now on again to Hardcastle Crags.

I had used all my water by this time so when I stopped at the
edge of the woodland for a brief boots-off break I drank about ½
pint of milk and had two of the custard cream biscuits (an evening

snack), that I had brought home from hospital last year. On again I went with refreshed feet along the woodland track. There will be masses of bluebells here next month; dog's mercury is flowering now. I took a photo of the woodland and one of the crags further on.

It was a long upward plod to Walshaw, slow but steady, and a good deal of height to regain. After Walshaw I had a pleasant surprise, seeing beside the walled track an unexpected streamlet of clear water so I had a good mugful. Soon the track reached open moorland and I was able to increase my pace and stride along it while enjoying views of the back of Boulsworth. (It must be the back, because when we lived at Colne I could see "the front" of Boulsworth from my bedroom window - it was 1701 feet according the map we had then). Where the track reaches the reservoirs it runs level for a few yards then the Pennine Way leads upwards again. Here at 5.35pm I decided to cool my feet with socks off before the final stage. A man came from the other direction and stopped for a chat about Ponden. At 5.45 I booted up and trod the flagstone way; the back of Boulsworth passed from my view. I saw a golden plover on Withins Height. Soon Top Withins appeared, sadly beheaded, with its group of trees - I reached it at 6.25pm. I strode on over flagstones or sandy, stony track to get down as soon as possible but missed a left turn (as did three other walkers seen at the pub) and I ended up walking along the road through Stanbury, where Val and Mick came out of the pub, the Old Silent Inn, and called to me. I said I'd walk down to Ponden Mill, Val with me, while Mick drove the van down. Up at the campsite I quickly pitched the tent, beside a single daffodil, while Val fetched water for me and we unpacked the food parcel they'd brought for me then we all went back to the pub until 9.50pm and had a pleasant evening together. Back at the tent I quickly cooked the meal of lentils and vegetables that I'd left soaking then washed feet and socks and had a late-ish night. This diary was written in the morning! Val and Mick were unable to walk with me, as they had originally hoped to, because Val's cat had to have drops in her eyes every six hours.

Tuesday 30th March 2004
- Ponden Hall to Gargrave, Eshton Road campsite:
At seven o'clock the sun shone on to the frost-covered tent and grass. After breakfast a man passed the tent and asked if he had

disturbed me in the night. "What time?" "About 2am." "No, I was sound asleep then." He said he was a night worker. Of course, instead of continuing directly from here on the Pennine Way, I had to go back round Ponden Reservoir to "connect up" with the route where I'd had a short lift with Val and Mick last night, then I continued along the road to the stile for the steep climb to Crag Bottom, then up the stone walled bridleway to the stile where I remember Paula stopping to cut a troublesome toenail when we walked the Pennine Way. The sun was shining from above but mist filled the valleys and covered the more distant hills. Further down the hill I'd taken a photo of a stone water trough near Crag Bottom and took another of Wolf Stones (443mtrs), with memories of Backpackers Club weekends I had arranged in that area - (Colne or Worsthorne to Cowling). It was lovely on the tops now; I was as happy as the singing skylarks, with curlews calling too. Between the flagstone stretches were sandy areas where the sun glinted on grains of quartzite. Too quickly this was over; I was down to Cowling and another upward effort was needed for Cowling Hill.

I stopped for lunch by a wall before reaching Lothersdale then continued past Woodhead Farm (where Paula and I had camped, with a warm welcome). The farm buildings are now houses, sadly. The path below Kirk Sykes Farm was not waymarked at the stile so I had a wander round two fields after taking the wrong stile - never mind - I soon reached the boggy top then continued up Pinhaw Beacon. Two ladies were descending but were so busy talking to each other about going to stay with one or the other that they noticed neither me nor the scenery - like three young men further north who were talking about work, of all things - surely they come to the hills to get away from work.

Boulsworth could be seen dimly in the mist from the top of Pinhaw Beacon - will it show on the photo? Pendle is hidden too. It was an easy walk after this down to Thornton in Craven, where I was ready to sit down by the time I had passed the houses but there was not time for a long break with some miles to go to Gargrave.

There were primroses on the south-facing hill out of Cowling but at Thornton there were masses of celandines, also dog's mercury, especially after Brown Farm. I had been told that there was no longer a PO/shop at Thornton but I knew there was at Gargrave. Easy fields and canal towpath were the terrain now, except for a ploughed field, path obliterated and footprints all over trying to find the way to the stile down the other side. A sign on the crest of the ridge would have helped, as would re-instating the path after ploughing. A short length of stony track after the canal was hard on the feet, then there were easy fields with Gargrave Church in sight. The Co-op Late Shop was open so I bought a pint of milk and a banana then made for the campsite in Eshton Road.

I remembered to get the LEJOG form signed before pitching, then put food to soak while I went for a wash - the lights were off at the shower block so a shower can wait until the morning. He only charged £1 for use of shower/hot water, no pitch fee as I was doing it for charity. After washing up I phoned Val, thanked her again for the food parcel, enquired after the cat and then I was ready for sleep. Today was 18½ miles; it will be an easier day tomorrow.

Wednesday 31ˢᵗ March
- Gargrave to Fountains Fell, Tennant Gill:

The sky was dark-clouded, threatening rain at 7.15am. I went and enjoyed a shower, with three convenient hooks for clothes and towel, and a mat to stand on! It must have been nearly eight o'clock when I had breakfast. Some mallards passed the tent. I wrote some of yesterday's diary so did not leave until 9.40am then I went into Gargrave to post two cards and to buy two more cards and stamps for Maurice and Trevor. A lane then field paths took me to Newfield Bridge, where I saw two oystercatchers. I'd seen mostly curlews until then. After the bridge I spoke to a couple stopped by a wall - it was sunny by now - then another man, from Brighouse, caught up. He was on a Pennine Way day walk and accompanied me to Malham. His was a more up-to-date map, showing the Pennine Way on the east of the river, not the west, so I have walked both. He said Wainwright gives the west route in his book. At Malham I found a tearoom at the Cove Centre, having found that the old café was closed, and I had a pot of tea with a slice of lemon and ginger cake and wrote Maurice's and Trevor's postcards then posted them. From the phone box I phoned Dad, who was not in, then Stella. On the way to Malham Cove I took a photo of a lamb with two ewes, then went up the steps to the top of the Cove, where I have stopped in warm sunshine to air my feet and eat a wholemeal teacake, yes, a good old wholemeal teacake with sardine and lettuce. I have had quite a long sunbathe so must now proceed to Malham Tarn.

There was still warm sunshine but a refreshingly cool breeze - just right for walking. There was lovely soft turf underfoot, a delight to walk on, until the stony track on the far side of the tarn. I sat on the bank here for a little while enjoying the peace, had a drink of water then I took a photo standing on the stones at the water's edge. I must look up the name of the fell behind the wood (on the photo). The track improved with a surface of fine chippings behind the house, then there was a gate and a sign for a path northward. Here it was sheltered from the breeze so the warmth made it necessary for me to remove a layer. There were even buds of milkwort showing on a limestone outcrop where I stopped. The curlew again was the bird of the day - I never tire of hearing the curlew - and, for a change, as I left Malham up the Cove road there were rooks making a fair amount of noise in the treetops by the beck.

A misleading sign made me continue north after a stile and along the lane, until I realised that it must have been pointing the wrong way and I should have gone up to the road back there. How many others have been confused here? That was an unnecessary ½ mile each way, so I went back to the Tennants Gill farm track (I'd turned the map over), up the track, past the farm then steeply upwards, pausing to drink the last of my water. The sun was dropping below Fountains Fell now but there was still plenty of daylight left and I was glad to reach the point where the path turned right and levelled out and became soft to the feet once more, but I was beginning to wonder when I should find Tennants Gill and water, when suddenly I heard the welcome sound of running water just ahead of me, where a lovely clear stream ran over pebbles. There was level ground with springy mat grass just above the path so I put down my rucksack, fetched water and quickly pitched, this time with the NW zip open as the light wind is from the SE. It was satisfying to arrive early enough for a good, long diary writing session, having enjoyed a meal of macaroni cheese with cauliflower and tomato followed by banana custard. The next thing is to wash self, underwear and socks; the thick ones dried well in today's sunshine, as did the Tracksters.

This was another really enjoyable day of about 15, mostly easy, miles, and now the breeze whispers in the grass and rushes; a curlew gives its bubbling song and the beck runs over the stones a few yards away.

Thursday 1ˢᵗ April
- Fountains Fell to Ling Gill Bridge:

The first sounds of the morning were a curlew calling, then a snipe, and then I heard a few spots of rain. This is a lovely spot, with beautiful clear water too. I slept a bit later than usual so it was 9.40am when I got moving, having taken a photo of the tent with Fountains Fell behind and discovered that it was the last exposure of that film so I nipped back into the tent to change the film before I finished packing. Today's walk started with a gradual ascent over the end of Fountains Fell with a cairn of the stone pillar type. This was in the foreground of the next photo, with the misty shape of Pen-y-Ghent behind. There were golden plover here too. I remembered the descending path from 20 years ago, with its rocky outcrop then easy, grassy track. On this grassy track I met six young people going the other way, to Malham, they said. Where the path met the lane I saw a snipe drop into the rushes but when I approached it flew off chipper-chippering, then I saw another one a minute or two later.

About 12 o'clock I was on the track towards the foot of Pen-y-Ghent and stopped to eat my apple - less to carry up the hill! - then on the other side of the stile I put on my Gore-Tex jacket, woolly hat and gloves, for the wind was getting colder and stronger. I enjoyed the rocky ascent, which didn't seem to take too long for one carrying about 30lbs weight, although I stopped and sat on a rock for a breather part way up, and I reached the summit soon after one o'clock, climbed over the stile and sat under the wall to have lunch like several others. Mandy from Harrogate and her friend John from Leeds came and sat beside me a couple of minutes later. Mandy was interested in LEJOG and my equipment. They both signed my sponsor form with £5 each, also tried on my Go-Lite Gust rucksack which they, like me, found heavy to lift but very comfortable on one's back. Mandy also gave me some cooked chicken and a banana left from her lunch, and would have given me a Satsuma, crisps and water if I'd wanted to carry the weight! I walked on a short way towards Plover Hill with them, then I had to cut off to the left to reach the edge path and Pennine Way descent. Near the base in a hollow were five men, three from Yorkshire and two from Suffolk, having their lunch. They asked what I was doing and the Yorkshiremen sponsored me. I romped on down to Horton-in-Ribblesdale with trouble-free knees. At the PO/shop I bought two postcards and a stamp, a tomato and three eggs, had a chat then went along the road to find the Pen-y-Ghent café closed. Never mind - that saved a bit of time - so I had a snack break with socks off beside the track up the hill from The Crown Inn. A few more spots of rain fell but stopped by the time I moved on at 3.45pm, at first steadily upward then the stony track varied between gently up, down or level. About a mile up the track I found a Gelert compass; I wonder why someone would have got out a compass while walking along a track. I shall have to contact TGO when I get home to have it put in the Lost and Found adverts. I keep my compass in map case. The Ribble Way forked off. On I went, until a stile in the wall appeared where no path is shown on the map. Have they diverted the Pennine Way? There seem to be fewer boot prints, but then it is stony so you wouldn't expect many. By my timing, I shouldn't turn off for half an hour. The map shows a wall on one side, a stream to ford, then turn off left. The ford eventually appeared, with a gate ahead and a signpost pointing left. Good! After another stop for water and chocolate I had to find a way through a horrendous mess of motorcycle tracks, which made great ruts over a wide area. I was cheered by curlew calls, and earlier a heron had flown up. Now down by Old Ings on a stony track again, which is hard on the feet, so I'll do as Geoff Boyling suggested and camp near Ling Gill Bridge. I see that there is now access to the Gill, but by a steep path, which I don't feel like tackling after a long day, so about 60 yards beyond the bridge here I am pitched beside the beck. My meal was delicious - dehydrated rice with extra water added, to mix with mushroom and garlic soup, then Mandy's roast chicken chopped and stirred in and topped with sliced tomato. Lovely, thank you, Mandy. This was followed by apple and strawberry crumble and custard. I am all washed and ready for bed so I'll have an early night then an early start for Hawes tomorrow. Another really enjoyable day of 15 miles.

Friday 2nd April
- Ling Gill Bridge to Great Shunner Fell, via Hawes:
It is the Anniversary of "the screws!" (the cannulated screws put in my leg last year) and a very happy day too, with much to be thankful for, although at 6.45am with rain pelting down on the tent I wondered what sort of day it would be. Instead of the intended early start I kept checking that things were in polythene bags, found

the new torch batteries and put them in, because the headtorch was getting quite dim last night. With waterproofs on and camera in the waterproof case, everything packed under cover, I went out to un-peg the flysheet - and the rain stopped - just like that!

By the time I was off it was 9.23, not too late, and it was not long before I got warm going up the hill in waterproofs so the Gore-Tex jacket came off quite soon. The first landmark was the Dales Way signpost pointing down to Cam Houses - I took a photo here - and just after that was the gate and wall where we had sat in a snowdrift for lunch, probably on the Pennine Way in 1983; I seem to remem-ber Trevor stirring some fruit drink powder into a mugful of snow to make a sort of slushy "ice lolly." I stopped about a mile after this for a banana (from Mandy!)

Now it was level walking for a fair distance and the sun was ap-pearing between the clouds. Even Ingleborough appeared briefly. The Pennine Way skirts Dodd Fell Hill - happy memories of when I took Joyce to Hawes, where she looked round while I popped up to the top, but now I walked at a good pace to give time in Hawes for a pot of tea and cake and buying food. However, I slowed down before I reached Gayle as my downhill muscles were aching slightly; I also stopped behind a wall for my brown teacake and herb pate. Fields of sheep and new lambs led to Gayle with its old stone houses and bridge then a footpath led to the church at Hawes - I took another photo here.

One of the first shops was "Elijah's" bakers for chocolate cara-mel slice and two wholemeal teacakes, then the adjoining grocers for a tin of sild, an apple and Wensleydale cheese with chives. The next stop was Hawes Tea Rooms with mouth-watering chocolate cake and a pot of tea, then I went on to the post office to post off a film and postcards and to buy two more postcards and a stamp. Finally I reached Outhwaite's Rope Works, where I looked around and took a photo of samples of church bell ropes. Now for a lei-surely walk along to the bridge and across the fields to Hardraw. As I walked I had an awful thought: I hadn't disposed of my rubbish bag in Hawes, but at Hardraw beside the phone box was a litter bin so the problem was solved and I had less weight to carry up Great Shunner Fell. I phoned Dad from here, as I'd had no mobile signal for a couple of nights. He had received his postcard.

The sun was shining brightly now for my walk up Great Shun-ner Fell. There was no hurry, just a steady pace, stopping here and there to enjoy the view - this was a really lovely walk and I am glad it was a few miles, giving more time to appreciate it. I reached the same height as Lovely Seat across the valley - memories of when I camped at Shivery Gill a few years ago while walking the Yoredale Way, just off the route, on the night before going up Lovely Seat (2,215 feet) - then I went on again up an easy gradient with sections of flagstones now and then in boggy bits, then it was a bit steeper before the last level stretch to the summit windshelter at 2,349 feet. I took a photo, of course, then I sat in the windshelter for some water and chocolate. In spite of a small notice asking people not to leave litter there was some foil, a fair sized piece, under a seat so I took this with me to dispose of later at a bin.

I planned to find a pitch on the way down after about a mile, where there was a stream, but before I got there a large dark cloud appeared to the east. I thought I heard thunder. After a few minutes the cloud was closer, then as I reached a small tarn the first heavy drops fell. Quickly, I went to the other, drier, side of the tarn, dropped the rucksack, pulled on the Gore-Tex jacket, quickly pitched the flysheet and put the rucksack and everything under it before pitching the inner. Now for water - a kettleful, bottleful and two pans full should do for tonight. The wind and rain lashed the tent but it was well pegged. I had some Wensleydale cheese crumbled over my lentils and vegetables, which was delicious.

Now, at 9.30pm, there has just been another lashing of rain but I'm snug in the sleeping bag with a nightlight burning cheerfully and a kettle of water ready for a wash. What a really lovely day, especially the sunny walk up the hill with hardly a breath of breeze, and views of hills all round, and memories of my previous times at the summit: the first was in snow, then once in wind and rain, then next time in hot weather. This time was perfect, an ideal celebration of the anniversary of "having the screws in my hip." 15½ miles today. The birds were golden plover, curlew, meadow pipit, lark and chaffinch.

Saturday 3rd April
- Great Shunner Fell to Frumming Beck, via Thwaite, Keld and Tan Hill Inn:

It is raining steadily and the cloud is down so that I can just see across the tarn but the whole summit "mound" of Great Shunner

Fell is hidden. I did various odd jobs to pass the time, being in no hurry to go out in that weather; it was windy too. When I did cool my hands by pulling out the cold pegs and rolling the wet flysheet I soon put on warm mitts then I got moving briskly back on to the Pennine Way at the nearby beacon cairn and down the rocky, boggy or flagged path. A farmer with his dog on a red quad cycle overtook me down the stony track. At Thwaite the shop no longer sold food; now it is attached to the pub and sells cards and gifts, but he did sell me one egg, in addition to a postcard, two stamps and a Mars bar. I posted Brian and Brenda's card and phoned Rose, who was wondering about my not being in contact so I explained that I'd had no mobile signal for three nights now - this will be the fourth. She is meeting me at the campsite at Middleton-in-Teesdale tomorrow; I said I hoped to be there about 2pm or soon after that.

Now time was getting on so I headed for the Pennine Way path, crossing a field of sheep and lambs then the Pennine Way climbed steeply up to another field to a corner near a barn where I took a photo looking back to Thwaite; it was brighter now. I remembered this high level route from previously on the Pennine Way, but I didn't remember that it took so long from Thwaite to Keld - perhaps it didn't, but today I had stopped to take off the Gore-Tex jacket and have a drink of water and take a photo, but there were stretches where care was needed - damp slippery stones or greasy mud to be wary of, although most of the path was fine with a lovely view down green, brown or wooded slopes to the River Swale in the valley bottom. The path began to rise before dropping to Keld and then crossed the bridge. At 1.40pm lunch was an urgent need. As I found a green spot under a tree by the lower waterfall large spots of rain began to fall, so waterproofs were pulled on quickly and I sat on the sit mat to munch my roll and chocolate caramel slice (from Hawes), leaving the apple until later. At 2 o'clock I was going steadily upward, then less steeply after passing the farm, with the wind behind me.

I thought I should reach Tan Hill Inn (1732ft) at about 4pm and, allowing for a slow pace over or through all the boggy bits; I actually arrived at 4.10pm. Earlier, blue sky had appeared ahead of me, but not for long, and when I actually saw Tan Hill Inn ahead I was pleased to have done so well, squelching gradually upward with some uphill and some level. I heard several golden plover and saw a couple of curlews and a snipe and there had been a chaffinch or two on the bridge over the beck in the field at Thwaite. When I entered the Inn they were all watching the Grand National. The choice of hot drinks was coffee or mulled wine. I had coffee but it was not good value at £1 for a small cup. Anyway, a sit down out of wind and rain gave added value and I wrote a postcard, of Hawes, to Joyce. Then I dressed up again in my waterproofs, and took a photo outside the pub before walking on.

The wind was stronger now, and behind me, but I think the rain had stopped. The path I remembered from 1983 with Paula - wet, boggy, with heather each side, just the same then as now. After a while a diversion sign directed the path along Frumming Beck, with mat grass here and there, still boggy in places but better than the first bit. By the time I'd almost reached the bridge over the beck, just ahead, leading to the track, I'd decided that I really had enough rough, boggy, uneven walking for the day. Just below was a levelish area, only boggy in parts, sheltered from the wind by the steep, high bank. It was just gone 6 o'clock - did I want to go further? No, I'd like to pitch here, but I'd have to be up early tomorrow. As I pitched the tent rain started to fall so I had made the right choice. With everything under cover I went to the beck for a supply of peaty water, then back to soak my food and unpack. I had a mug of tea, the rest of a packet of cream of mushroom soup, dehydrated lentils with broccoli, carrot and red pepper in garlic and herb sauce then dehydrated fruit salad - Kiwi fruit, strawberries, nectarine and pear with cold custard. It was all very nice and satisfying.

The rain, I think, has pattered down all evening. I have washed self, socks and underwear and I'm sitting cosily in the sleeping bag with a nightlight beside me. I have checked tomorrow's route on the map, written the diary, so I shall listen to the radio (Classic FM) for a little while before settling down. Today was only 13 miles, not easy ones and I'd started late, but it was a satisfying day.

Sunday 4th April 2004
- Frumming Beck to Middleton -in-Teesdale:
It was a clear sky at 6.30 this morning; at 7 o'clock the sun came over the hill and shone into the tent. I took a photo of the tent, looking south-west before moving off just after half past eight. I made good time, getting to Trough Heads, my original destination for last night, in an hour so I stopped for a drink of water and a bit of chocolate. This first hour was along a moorland track with sheep, curlew and

lapwing then, after Sleightholme, the Pennine Way crosses a couple of fields to a footbridge then up steeply to a high grassy bank above the beck. Several rabbits lolloped off. The path across the moor from Trough Heads on the map is straight but this one went right and left before heading down to God's Bridge where, of course, the sun went in when I took a photo. The way climbs past a house then a signs tells you to go left for 200 yards for the underpass under the A66, where you emerge to a lot of litter, unfortunately, then once more there are some boggy miles, pleasant undulating ones with larks, golden plover, grouse and curlew. After crossing a footbridge over Deepdale Beck the path ascends again on more grassy terrain to 427 metres at Race Yate then there is a view over a gate to another watershed, Balderhead and Blackton Reservoirs.

It was an easy walk down - I was at Clove Lodge by 12.20, but I was confused at Birk Hat where Hannah Hauxwell used to live. There were no signs or waymarks for the Pennine Way, and a tarmac drive was where a footpath was shown on the map. Should one go through the gate or was it private property? I followed arrows along the reservoir but soon realised that was wrong and half an hour wasted, well not really wasted but I had to meet Rose and this made me half an hour later. I returned to the garden gate at Birk Hat. Was that a faint, white PW on a stone a few yards inside? (There were no problems here 20 years ago). It was PW, so through the gate and up the drive I went, to the lane and across to the sign and stile for the next section of the way. This was fine until some farm buildings and a stile telling you to keep to the path in single file, but no path was visible so I used the compass to head in the right direction towards How. The wind now came in strong gusts; I preferred it behind me so I turned along the lane for a couple of miles. Also a phone was shown on the map so I could phone Rose and tell her that I'd be a bit late. However, no phone was there now. The field path to Mickleton was a delight - easy to walk with way-marked stiles, green underfoot and going where it should go! I saw the old railway bridge ahead and wondered if the track was walkable, then saw two people walking there! It led towards Middleton-in-Teesdale to the Lonton Lane, leaving just a little of the B6277 to take me to the campsite where Rose was waiting in her tent - I'd arrived about 3.45pm. It was good to see her and she gave me my food parcel. The afternoon remained showery. I forced myself later on to leave my sleeping bag and go for a refreshing shower and do some washing - I hope it dries! I also managed to get sufficient phone signal to phone Anita but had no success with one or two other attempted phone calls.

14 miles was today's total.

Monday 5th April
- Middleton-in-Teesdale to Knott Hill Farm:

It took quite a while to pack this morning, dealing with the food parcel contents and wet washing. I put the rest of the Wensleydale cheese and half a tomato in a granary roll for lunch - Rose and I had done some shopping at the Co-op, including some Fairtrade chocolate. When we set off I dropped the shower key through the letterbox as requested. The weather was heavy showers and sunny spells. Rose wanted to buy a sit mat, having forgotten hers, and I wanted to post some maps home and buy a postcard so it was late when we eventually got on to the Pennine Way, which did not matter because today was originally planned to be an easy five miles to Holwick, because Rose had not backpacked for some time, although we had discussed going on to just before Falcon Clints. After each shower we were interested to see how quickly our warm mitts dried out in the sun. I took a photo of Rose by the River Tees with a craggy rock behind her - it was actually sunny then - then she took one of me on my camera near Low Force. Before this we followed a track off route to an old barn and sheltered there - lovely with its long wooden rack of sweet-smelling hay down one wall and a little window at the end with knots of pink binder twine on the sill. We saw lots of rabbits during the day. Near High Force I pitched my flysheet between the juniper bushes to give shelter for lunch and it actually dried out. We continued to Cronkley, sheltering during another wintry shower in an old railway wagon with a rotting floor, until blue sky drew us out and onward. On seeing the Tees as we crossed the bridge we decided that the path beside it was probably flooded so we headed up a rather muddy footpath with some awkward gates then across some fields.

As we approached the small white buildings of Knott Hill Farm I suggested to Rose that we could ask to camp there as the wind was increasing in strength. Rose was delighted that we were allowed to pitch here - charge £2 each, grid ref 858300. We have settled in a field corner with wall shelter where the wind whistles loudly, telling us what we are missing! The lady here, Mrs Stevenson, says that we can come in the back door and through to the bathroom; she had said that drinking water was "down there" at the front, which appeared to be in the shippon with a few cows and two calves.

Now back to the tents for a good hot meal - macaroni cheese and cauliflower, then I almost dropped asleep while writing the diary....this is being finished in the morning after a warm, comfortable night. The wind is quieter and there are occasional spatters of rain. There are calls of lapwing and curlew and pheasant, and a snipe drumming and chittering. Due to the wind we are going to avoid the Pennine Way over the high tops of Little Dun Fell, Great Dun Fell and Cross Fell, instead going past Cow Green Reservoir and over towards Garrigill, saving a day possibly. After all, I have walked the complete Pennine Way years ago and I am still walking from Land's End to John O'Groats so it does not matter what route I use. Strong winds are best avoided!

Tuesday 6th April
- Knott Hill Farm, Teesdale, to Garrigill:
I slept until 7.25 this morning, and Rose had switched off her alarm so didn't call me, which made us a bit late. However, it was cloudy with some rain. I took a photo of the white Knott Hill Farm from the field corner with the tents in the foreground. Nobody was about when we went to the house to use the bathroom, but I saw a card by the telephone which told us that her name was Mrs Stevenson, of Knott Hill, Forest in Teesdale, so thank you very much Mrs Stevenson for the very welcome pitch sheltered from the wind! It must have been about 10.20am when we started walking along the farm track then turned left over the bridge over the now very wide River Tees, then a bridleway and a footpath by the river, where oyster-catchers were calling, led to the lane.

After two miles of lane (today part of it was closed - to traffic - for one day a year, by Raby Estates) we came to a small building with boarded up windows. The door opened to show a small bothy-type room with a fireplace but no bunks or furnishings, and a horrible mess of rubbish, plastic containers of milk and even some unused soups, coffee sachets and hot chocolate. We tried to tidy up. I took one sachet of hot chocolate, left the other usable packets on the "mantelpiece" and wrote a note saying "Please take your rubbish

THE RAIN STOPPED SOON AFTER LAND'S END

ON BODMIN MOOR APPROACHING BROWN WILLY

ROS AND JULIA ON THE COTSWOLD WAY

SHELTERED FROM THE WIND BY FRUMMING BECK

THE SUMMIT OF LAMMER LAW, LAMMERMUIRS

EARLY MORNING ON EAST LOMOND

GLEN TILT NEAR THE FALLS OF TARF

THRIFT AND VERNAL SQUILL AT DUNCANSBY STACKS

away with you! Do you think it is a welcome sight when you come in?"

Still, we appreciated shelter from the rain that had persisted all morning and somewhere to stop for a drink of water and a piece of flapjack. We walked past Cow Green Reservoir and I took a rainy photo looking across it. We continued along the track then I saw on the map "mine (dis)" towards the far end and went on ahead to the buildings - a couple of open shed-type stone buildings and a small cottage type building, again with boarded up windows. I tried the latch - once more the door opened, revealing a table and benches this time, so I deposited my rucksack on a bench and went to meet Rose. She was delighted at this luxury lunch shelter and we sat at the table with our food. She got out her mini Trangia for soup so heated enough water for my hot chocolate too - the hot mug helped to dry damp mitts. It was a case of having the door open, with a draught, for light, or the door shut, to be warmer in darkness. We lit a small candle that we found there, then Rose realised that she had three bigger ones so lit them all, making it warm and cheerful. As we packed to leave I said to Rose, "Some people say 'Thank God' and don't mean it, but for this shelter I can say it and really mean it." It made such a difference in that weather.

We came out to a spell of bright sunshine and walked along the now grassy track with alternating showers of rain or hail and sunshine. Little and Great Dun Fells and Cross Fell were all white-topped now, and would have been even more windy than it was here. My suggestion had been to go across country for about a mile to join the track to Garrigill, then Rose pointed out that with all the rain the stream crossings might not be possible, so that left the B6277 Alston road. Much as I dislike road walking, I saw the sense of this and there was very little traffic at all for the three miles we were on it. At one point a lay-by had a post and rail fence; Rose was ready to sit down and the sun was shining so I put my flysheet and T-shirt over the fence to dry for about ten minutes while we sat down for a drink of water and a snack. Soon after this, opposite a milestone, a path led down to Hole House Farm. Rose would have liked to camp here as her feet were hurting but nobody was in to ask and no water tap visible so we continued up the other side to a track, then I went ahead to ask at Lee House, where we were told we could go down over the fence to the river bank and either carry water or get it from the stream flowing into the River South Tyne.

We used stream water to save carrying it down from the house. This was after 11 miles walk that day and was a pleasant spot high on the river bank, about a mile before Garrigill, next to a field of sheep and lambs.

Wednesday 7th April
- near Garrigill to Maiden Way, between Slaggyford and Lambley:

At about 6.45am I woke and soon afterwards heard the farmer (it was his shepherd, actually) chugging about the field on his quad cycle. More than a few spots of rain fell so we packed damp tents again then left our pleasant pitch, climbed over the fence, walked up the fields, past the house to the lane and down to Garrigill. There was a convenient litterbin, a phone box where I phoned Dad and the Post Office/shop was open. I bought a raspberry yoghurt to eat straight away and two eggs; Rose bought a pie. It was now that we met the farmer again, who asked if his shepherd has disturbed us this morning. The Pennine Way out of Garrigill is mostly a lovely riverside walk along the South Tyne. Butterbur was the only flower that we saw along there. The path crossed a footbridge then left the river to take us over stiles of varying degrees of difficulty, such as a step stile with a wooden post to swing round between two steps. The last stretch into Alston was a high-level path above the river and past the Youth Hostel.

We had made it by 1pm but Rose wanted to leave her rucksack at the TIC and make some enquiries there - it was unbearably hot in there so I went on up the street and left my rucksack outside the Blueberry Café in the corner, having told Rose that I'd see her there, and found an outdoor shop next door so, as Rose had not appeared, I nipped in for a new pair of overtrousers since mine had a five inch tear, the result of a rubbed inside leg giving a half inch split that had caught on barbed wire while I was getting over a stile. Then Rose came in and wanted to buy something (shoes) - why couldn't we have lunch first then she could buy things while I walked on, since she was going home today? While she was trying them on I went to the Co-op across the road and bought a carrot, a tomato, 2 apples, milk, 4 rolls, a tin of chopped ham and pork and a packet of mash, then returned to find Rose trying on some trousers. At last we had lunch! I had lentil and vegetable soup and a roll then coffee and walnut cake and a pot of tea. Lovely. Then I asked Rose to take a photo of me at the market cross where, years ago, I had taken one of Paula and Trevor, then we said Goodbye and I proceeded down to the TIC to buy a postcard and ask about the disused railway as a route. They said that you could walk beside the narrow gauge railway from the signal box to the end then continue along the track to Slaggyford. I also asked which villages had shops - surprisingly they did not know!

After the railway ended this was a nice, dry (mostly, anyway) grassy track with easy walking and pleasant views of the South Tyne valley. At Slaggyford I posted a card, written in sunshine along the railway, and saw a sign "Cycleway - 8 miles to Lambley." The problem was finding a way off the railway after Knarsdale to join the Pennine Way, which was the Maiden Way at that point, but I did eventually after the sharp road bend, by going up a steep bracken bank, stepping over a low wire fence, as others had done obviously, then finding a path, which I assume is the Pennine Way but it is off my map now and the other map is in my pack.

It must have been gone 7 o'clock when I found water and I was certainly ready to stop then - my right shoulder was aching a bit with the extra weight. Now I am well fed and tired so I shall settle down and listen to the curlew and lapwing calls around me.

Thursday 8th April
- Maiden Way to Hadrian's Wall:

Curlew calls continued during the early part of the night. Frost on the tent in the morning was a surprise as I'd been so warm and comfortable on the soft bed of mat grass and moss. Breakfast was Puffed Wheat with fresh milk then fried chopped ham and pork with egg. At 9.10am I set off along the Maiden Way with the company of lapwing, curlew, golden plover, grouse and meadow pipit. The path was quite boggy at first then better drained when it sloped down over grass. The Pennine Way departed from my route by a stile on the left and I went straight on down for the road to Lambley and the lane to Lambley Farm, opposite which is a bridleway then a footpath through fields of sheep and lambs where a farmer called a cheerful "Hello." I stopped further on by the river for an apple and spread my towel over the wire fence - it would be nice to have a dry one. I am carrying it over the rucksack today.

The path continued to a woodland area alongside a stream to a footbridge then more woodland by the South Tyne, very attractive with greater woodrush and wood anemones. I stopped again higher up in the wood to change my film so decided to write a bit of the diary then. I heard but did not see the "Veni, Vidi, Vici" bird high in the trees.

After Bridge End I took a photo of the bridge and a ewe and lamb from the farm track, then proceeded through the muddy farmyard and path - it was not surprising that it was muddy after all the rain in the last two days - then the path improved as it led past gorse bushes and up between the trees to a field or two, then another farm track where I removed my overtrousers before going along the footpath into Haltwhistle, where I bought an apple and banana and two postcards. I posted off a film then went in Pillar Box Café for a pot of tea and delicious big slice of chocolate cake, then went to the Post Office next door for stamps.

Now I was ready to head for Hadrian's Wall and made my way up the lane. At a bend I remembered that it was here in 1984 that Paula, Trevor and I, with Rusty, met a lady who said, "Hasn't he got bonny colours!" Trevor called Rusty "Bonny Colours" for some time after that. From the lane I joined a track, with a few daffodils beside it, to a field path and, at last, the Wall.

At Milecastle 42 I took a photo, then continued up and down, meeting several people, two of them walking the whole Wall from Newcastle. It was more strenuous than I remembered but the choc-olate cake fuelled me! I didn't need my cheese roll until 5.15pm! Crag Lough was lovely; the path now leads between pines on the north side of the wall, but after going up Hotbank I was feeling a bit tired. The path now descended to leave Hadrian's Wall where the Pennine Way leads northward. As I came down the grassy path away from the Wall on the crags I saw a spring and a trickle of water flowing down towards rushes. Ah! Water! I took my pack back up towards the crags, went back down to fill the water bag, kettle and a Platypus bottle, and then pitched the tent. I was ready to stop and just under the Wall was an atmospheric spot. The map hadn't told me that there was water here.

The kettle was soon on and a meal cooked, then I had the plea-sure of an answerphone message from Joy, so I phoned her. She wished me a happy birthday for tomorrow and we had a chat then I phoned Dad and Lynette. It has been a good day of about 14½ miles and it was nice to have had no rain. It is satisfying to have got so far - now North of the Wall, just. Now it's time for a wash and bed.

GOOD FRIDAY 9th April
- Hadrian's Wall to Bellingham:

At 7.20am I said "Happy Birthday" to myself! Soon after this raindrops pattered on the flysheet. Breakfast was wheatflakes with fresh milk, baked beans, toast and tea, then I put some cheese in a roll ready for my lunch. It was nice to use a dry towel, after yesterday's drying on the rucksack. Although the Wall and crags are misty now I think it was a marvellous place to pitch. I shall be testing the new overtrousers today...and an hour later I was too hot in them and the rain had stopped.

Not long after I started walking, perhaps at the second stile, a man in a red jacket caught up with me. He is doing the Pennine Way in stages; this section was arranged by taking his bike to Byrness by car, driving to Housesteads I think, walking from Housesteads to Byrness and cycling back to his car. Judging by his pack size, he was not backpacking. He said he'd get on when I stopped to remove waterproofs, which was just as well for I couldn't go at that pace all day with about 30lbs to carry, especially uphill. Here we were on forest track, misty with not a lot to see but I took a photo anyway, the previous one being the tent under Hadrian's Wall. Later on the Pennine Way left the forest on crunchy stones, recently laid, for marshy fields. I stopped under a tree for a snack at 11.40 then went on to Wark Burn for lunch near the footbridge at one o'clock. It was a peaceful spot. Since it was my birthday I had an Eccles Cake as an extra and checked the phone for messages but there was no signal here. From the bridge I took a photo of the burn, then a few minutes later up the path there was a bank of primroses, masses of them, so I took another photo. The primroses and the larks singing were real birthday treats - larks singing, curlews calling and lapwings - lovely.

I called the man in the red jacket "Wilmslow Man" as that was where he came from, and noticed from time to time "Wilmslow Man's" footprints, fresh ones, the only ones going this way. Up, along, and down to the Houxty Burn I went, over another footbridge and another over a stream then up to Shitlington Hall. I changed to the next map here - another step forward. More fields and mud, not too bad, then up to Shitlington Crags, which I remembered reaching in rain in 1984 with P. & T. I stopped for an apple then took a photo of the rocky way up, which I had forgotten. A track brought me to a gateway where a sign gave details of Demesne Farm Campsite,

Bellingham. Showers - Ah, that would be nice, although I had intended to go on until 6.30pm and I should be at Bellingham by five or soon after. However, an early, leisurely pitch and a shower would be nice, especially on my birthday. Yes, a shorter day of about 13 miles is all right, as I am still half a day ahead.

A mile or so of road takes the Pennine Way into Bellingham; the Bellingham sign has daffodils around, or in front of it. The Late Shop was open so I bought fresh milk, a pear and a cheese scone before going to the farm, where the farmer was actually at the gate. Yes, they did do camping 20 years ago, and yes, I could camp - no charge - and he signed the LEJOG form. I only had to pay 20p for the shower, but a shower was what I wanted. I pitched over by the hedge near another small tent, unpacked, went for a refreshing shower and washed my thin socks, having left food soaking. The kettle went on for tea and soup, and then there was macaroni cheese with cauliflower and leek, and fruit salad and Dream Topping.

I phoned one or two people to thank them for their birthday messages. I omitted to say that I stopped for a break after Lowgill (with the friendly dogs), sat on a bank under a Pennine Way signpost at about 2.45pm and switched the phone on to find birthday greetings from Maurice and Julie, Anita & Paul, and Will, also one from a number I didn't recognise, which I later found out was Trevor. That was really nice to have messages actually on my birthday since I can't have cards on my travels.

Now I've had a chat with the man from the next tent, Martin Wilson, who has been cycling round Kielder. He is interested in the Backpackers Club. It has been a lovely day, not a lot of sun, but still really lovely with birthday messages, larksong and primroses.

Saturday 10th April
- Bellingham to Blakehopeburnhaugh:
After a comfortable and peaceful night I woke at twenty past seven to find no other campers up and about, not even Martin in the next tent, but we had a chat after breakfast and I gave him details of the Backpackers Club (the address of the Membership Secretaries). He also used to ride and once beat Mark Phillips! Anyway, after talking for some time I did not get away until ten past ten, then after a mile or so I felt sure that I'd given him the Shiners' address as Solihull not Selly Oak, but I've told Anne Ling tonight and she'll e-mail

them with his address. Also in the first mile I came upon four young men with rucksacks and maps, standing talking. They said they had done, or were doing, 25 miles in three days. Today a third of that would surely have been enough with all the bogginess! When I last looked back before Hareshaw House they were still some way behind me, having followed the posts through the fields. I stopped on the other side of the farm track to phone Malcolm & Margaret and Jim & Maggie while there was a signal. There is dampness in the air and grey clouds all round but no proper rain, and it was not wet all day, except underfoot!

Lord's Shaw, where I'd thought I'd have a possible pitch after Bellingham originally, had a suitable area for a tent but no convenient water - my lunch stop, just before going up the hill, had water. Here I met the only walker of the day going south from Byrness to Bellingham. I had also seen "Wilmslow Man's" footprints ahead of me. "Byrness Man" told me it was very boggy ahead - too true! Apart from the ascent of Padon Hill on a good surface, there was a very long, boggy paddle. You go on squelching through pools, peat, rushes and sphagnum moss trying to dodge the worst wet bits. It seems that forestry vehicles have used the path. It took longer than expected so I was relieved to reach the forest track and could look at the hills ahead instead of having eyes to the ground all the time. Logs were piled beside the track - some were numbered up to 25 and one batch had FC on one log and "poom" on another; I wondered about this for a few minutes until I realised that it was "wood" upside-down! Obvious though.

About 5.50pm I reached Blakehopeburnhaugh so I took a photo of the picnic table where, 20 years ago, Trevor had been delighted by the chaffinches landing to pick up crumbs as we sat having our lunch. I also filled a water bottle and was heading for the "official" wild pitch, that I'd seen a few years ago, but after going up 22 steps on the Three Kings Walk my legs said "Enough" at the top, where there is a round sheepfold. I pitched here on soft grass and moss, fetched more water from the stream at the bottom of the steps, and then cooked a meal. Today was only 13 ½ miles but I was definitely slowed down by all the bog-plodding. However, it was a good day and I made progress. I am looking forward to the Cheviots tomorrow, also waking to hear birds in the surrounding trees. I did not notice any birds today - I'm sure there were some but I was concentrating on where to put my feet.

EASTER SUNDAY 11th April 2004
- Blakehopeburnhaugh to Cheviots:

Several times during the night tawny owls called, the t-whit and the t-whoo, very near. Once I heard a rustle and found that a used tea bag had been nibbled and before that I'd heard a clink - I had oats soaking for porridge, the pan covered by a foil plate, weighted with the pan grip. There was no sign of the culprit when I unzipped the tent but I brought the pan into the inner to keep it safe. There are not as many birds as I expected this morning; a wren sang loudly and another bird sounded like "I really DO want to come with you." It is still and peaceful and green in this circle of moss and bilberry and the surrounding old stone wall with its moss and lichen. Happy Easter! My Easter egg was a boiled brown egg, and an Eccles Cake to follow was something else with which to celebrate. In a way, I don't want to move from here but at the same time I'm eager to enjoy the wild Cheviots ahead so I'll finish packing.

Down the twenty two steps again, then I retraced my steps between the trees to the Pennine Way and continued to Byrness. A tiny cross on the map marked a tiny church beside the way, surrounded by daffodils. A notice on the door said that services today were at Elsdon and Otterburn; the service at Byrness was on the first Sunday of the month, so I went to a church on Easter Day but not to a service. I took a photo from round the back, where it was sunny, with the daffodils.

A long, steep path leads upward, as I remembered, between the evergreens, requiring a few "breathers." This is one of the steepest parts of the Pennine Way. At last it emerges between grey rocks then there is a short scramble on to the ridge. How good to be up there. The green path led away over the hilltops; larks sang and two birds swooped low over the grass and were gone. Were they the first swallows? The grassy path rolled onwards, occasionally boggy or, in one place, there were wooden boards and in others it was stone-flagged. This was an area I remembered well - Windy Rigg was windy in 1984 but not today. The sun broke through now and then so I removed the warm North Cape top. I stopped to sit on the rocks and eat an apple but my intended lunch spot was near the gate below Chew Green Roman Camps, where Paula, Trevor and I had pitched the old Romany tent 20 years ago, and heard the gate banging and squeaking in the wind that night. I reached this spot to find the water clear and fresh - I had a mugful then put the flysheet to dry and sat down, boots and socks off, to tuck into cheese and tomato roll, fruitcake and Grasmere Ginger-bread. It was lovely to sit there in the sun and remember our previous visit when, on Chew Green Camp, a lamb approached Rusty, mistaking him for its Mum!

Eventually I packed up and booted up, although in no hurry. The route went up and down over Black Halls and Lamb Hill, with the Refuge Hut at Yeavering Bell enticing me in for a snack - two others were just leaving and two more walkers had just left. The map showed accessible water just after Mozie Law, also on Windy Gyle. Mozie Law would do for tonight's pitch; there was plenty of time to enjoy Windy Gyle tomorrow. I remembered the fence corner just before Mozie Law, where Paula, Trevor and I had had lunch in a chilly breeze sitting on a log - there was nowhere else dry in the peat to sit. That could have been the same log, lying by the border fence, and now stone flags eased the way over the peat-bog area. A movement caught my eye to the right - a wild Cheviot goat. I took a photo although the goat was not very near. From here the path gently descended to a stile and my planned and hoped-for pitch. What was more, there was a trickle of a stream in the bottom, before the one shown on the map, so there was no distance to walk for water; I was able to drop the pack, fetch water, pitch and cook my meal, which was turkey, with peas, carrots and courgette in garlic and herb sauce with mash. There was actually a phone signal and a message from Bryan Crick but I had to change the battery before replying. At last I got round to washing self and socks before lighting the nightlight. What a lovely day it has been; I'm looking forward to another wild hilly day tomorrow.

14½ marvellous miles!

EASTER MONDAY 14ᵀᴴ April
- Windy Gyle to Town Yetholm:
The sun shone on the tent at seven o'clock so up I got and out on to a guyline went the underwear, socks and tea towel to dry. Muesli, baked beans, toast and tea were my breakfast, accompanied by larksong - the larks were singing before I actually made a move out of the sleeping bag. The blue sky is streaked with grey cloud now. I have washed up but I can't get a weather forecast because I forgot to turn a radio battery around so it must have rubbed against something, got switched on and drained the battery.

This is one of the loveliest wild pitches, with not a sound but the larks and the occasional curlew. After the one or two goats that I saw yesterday I saw another small group, just on the edge of the hill, Mozie Law, but there was little contrast against the dark moorland vegetation for them to show up on a photo. I shall now have to pack up and leave this delightful spot but it will remain in my memory.

The path led round the hillside then upward and away towards the border fence, boggy in places, as of old, and flagged in places, up Windy Gyle, where there was now a signpost. After taking a photo I strode on, enjoying the wildness of the hills, and the peace, meeting only three cyclists, about 10.30am, pushing their cycles, and then one walker. We each said that the other was the first walker that we'd seen today, Easter Monday. It was quite a boggy pull up to Auchope Cairn so I stopped for a breather and a drink of water while two more walkers passed en route for The Cheviot.

The skylarks were still the most numerous birds today, with meadow pipits and a grouse or two, and twice I heard golden plover - I love their soft, whistling calls. I pressed on, now with memories of the snow at Auchope Cairn in 1984, but I had forgotten how long the descent was to the old railway wagon, which was now replaced by a Mountain Refuge Hut on this side of the fence - before we had pitched the old Ultimate Romany tent between fence and railway wagon for shelter, for even the three of us had not been able to slide the door open, due to its runners being frozen we supposed. I had planned to have lunch here; this was a late one at 1.35pm. As I approached the hut I saw a movement behind it so went round the front to see a golden plover walk away through the fence to where the wagon had been. Happy memories again.

Next came The Schil (605 metres); it was quite a pull up here so I had a couple of pauses for breath and to look back at the hut, already looking distant, and Auchope Cairn and the Cheviot. It is surprising how soon hills and other landmarks, once far ahead, so quickly recede into the distance, but it is nice to look back and see them before looking ahead to the next horizon. I had forgotten that the summit of The Schil was rocky.

I dropped down away from the old views to new ones of green sheep pasture. There were the ruins of Old Halterburn and then another farm was bypassed by the Pennine Way going over a foot-bridge and alongside a field. Here lay the remains of an egg with a ¾ inch hole in the side where an animal or bird had eaten the contents. Back on the track were horses' hoof prints. Celandines grew on the verge and a black cow licked her calf's head and neck as they lay in the sunshine. The track became lane and a sign for Pennine Way and St Cuthbert's Way was at the lane-side. It was not far now to Kirk Yetholm but the last mile seemed a long one, although I arrived about twenty minutes earlier than I had expected.

At the Border Inn I asked, as Bryan Crick had suggested on the phone last night, if I qualified for the Wainwright's half pint, explaining that I had not claimed it when I completed the Pennine Way in 1984 but now, on LEJOG, I had not walked the full Pennine Way from Edale but had joined it at Wessenden Head. At first he seemed a bit doubtful whether I qualified - I said it was up to him - but he let me have it, in cider too, which I said I'd prefer. While I was sipping it at leisure with pack removed, the man at the next table asked about the walk. He also mentioned that a friend of his had a green wooden holiday cabin up the lane - had I seen it? Yes, I had - beautiful with lots of daffodils and a bright green lawn. He said the fishing here was not much good now because so much fertiliser and pesticide ran off the fields into the river.

I rose from the table at ten to six and enquired about evening meals, as I had no dehydrated meal with me for tonight. Those meals in the waiting parcel were for the days ahead. Served from 6.30pm I was told, so I said I might be back......until I reached Rex and Sue's house at Town Yetholm (they were not able to be there but had kindly let me have the keys) and found a note taped to the blue front door asking if I'd like to come round for a meal, from Stuart and Carolyn next door. I went straight there before unlocking the door and accepted their kind invitation - in half an hour would be all right - and Stuart came round to make sure that it wasn't too difficult to turn the water on. The kettle went on for a mug of tea; the immersion heater went on for a bath later. Then I had a quick wash and change into clean clothes, putting the clothes I had been wearing to soak until I returned.

What nice people! There was sherry and apple juice to drink, then a starter of pink and white grapefruit (and "Have some more!") followed by steak and mushroom casserole with broccoli and mash ("Have some more!") then cherry crumble and thick "Scots" custard, after which we sat by the log fire for cups of tea. We talked about walking, Northumberland, churches, birds - all sorts - and time passed quickly. I had to tear myself away when I saw that it was 10.45pm, to go and finish my washing while the bath water was running. It felt good to have a relaxing bath - I nearly went to sleep in it - and the toenails needed a cut too. I was soon settled in the sleeping bag on the Z-Rest on the living room floor and slept well until seven o'clock after another really enjoyable day.

Tuesday 12th April 2004
- Town Yetholm to Greenlaw, via Kelso:

I decided to have my porridge and boiled egg first and then have a wash and wash my hair, just finishing off one of the mini-bottles of shampoo that I'd started a few days ago at Middleton-in-Teesdale. That felt better. Packing took almost the same time as when camping because the Z-rest had to go in first, then the food bag; meths was poured into its container/bottle and the dry, washed clothes packed in their bag. I checked that I had not left anything. Before leaving I went to the Post Office to post maps home and to buy stamps, then to the shop for a postcard for Tony Wilson, and two morning rolls and an apple. Now I could get my boots on and get in harness.

I modified the route slightly to reduce the length now that there was the extra weight of food from the parcel, but I still think it was 19-20 miles to Greenlaw, about ten of these being to Kelso. Most of the route was along narrow lanes with green verges. Beside one or two lanes grew the white flowers of three-cornered leek, or something very like it, which I remembered from the Isles of Scilly in 2001. There were also red and white dead nettles, speedwell, colts-foot, lots of celandines but only a couple of primroses, as well as lots of daffodils. Birds today were: blackbirds, chaffinches, yellowhammers, sparrows, rooks and "Veni, Vidi, Vici" bird plus chiffchaff and one curlew, also plenty of pheasants.

Today's walking was different, with a sunny morning and a more cloudy afternoon; there were lanes with little traffic except hurrying tractors, fields full of sheep or a horse or two, or young cattle or ploughed fields with green shoots of cereal crops coming up. Where gorse bushes grew in the hedgerows they had been trimmed to the shape of the hedges, making large patches of yellow. Farm buildings varied from red sandstone to gigantic factory-like barns. A lady spoke as she left a farm on a bicycle with a sheepdog running beside her. Kelso was a pleasant town where I should have liked to spend more time; perhaps I should have stopped at the campsite and had an afternoon of exploration then had a shorter day tomorrow, but I was eager to get on. I bought a delicious filled brown roll and some carrot cake from Rothbury Bakery, the shop recommended by Stuart and Carolyn, and ate them while sitting on a seat in the square. After this I bought three eggs at a butcher's then it was time to walk on and head for Greenlaw. Eventually I came over the final hill to see Greenlaw below and an expanse of caravans higher up. The map has a tent sign too, so no worries about seeing only caravans. It looked a big site.

The village shop was open so I bought fresh milk, chocolate, a banana and a pear, and then went up round the corner to the site. Reception was closed but a phone number was given, so I used the mobile phone although it was before seven. A man said he would be there in five minutes. I explained that I was doing Land's End to John O'Groats and that I had a small backpacking tent - how much would it be for one night? "Tents £10." "But even at the most luxurious site I've been to (Kingsbury Water Park) they charged £4 for Backpackers." "Shall we say £5 then?" "Some even say there's no need to pay if you're doing it for charity." "Oh, that's all right then. What charity are you doing it for?"

He gave me a key and told me to turn right after crossing the bridge. What a long walk! A stony track led to the bridge, another stony track round a central grassy area where children were playing and at the end was space beside an unoccupied caravan near the river. Mine was the only tent on the touring field. Anyway, I was hungry after my long walk so a mug of tea and a meal were needed and enjoyed first, then I discovered, after a long walk of perhaps a ¼ mile back to the shower block, "No hot showers after 8.30pm." At least I could wash my underwear, socks and feet in hot water and leave the shower until the morning. As I settled into the sleeping bag all was peaceful on the site; the caravan next to me was unoccupied and all I could hear was the sound of the river below.

Wednesday 14ᵗʰ April 2004
- Greenlaw to Watch Water, Southern Upland Way:
Hot showers, the notice said, were available from eight to ten a.m. Not very convenient, so that meant that I had to have breakfast first, wash up, put sardines and tomato in my rolls and then go for a shower. It was such a distance to and from the shower block that I was late setting off. Next I went to the shop for some lunch items: a

couple of rolls, some chocolate caramel shortbread (in a round foil plate that would be useful later as a pan lid) and new batteries for the radio before heading northwards; it would have been about half past ten when I left the shop.

The route was back up the road past the caravan park. At the gateway into woodland I stopped to take a grey-skied photo looking back to Greenlaw. A grassy track with red soil and stones each side led enticingly onward past the old trees and gorse bushes, but then appeared to turn slightly left where I expected a right fork. Perhaps it would revert to that direction later - there were hoof prints going both ways on this track. This was not right at all, although the walking had been pleasant, and I ended up at a gate on to the moor roughly where Heriots Dyke is marked on the map, but there was no sign of either path - the one I followed north seemed to be a sheep trod which led, eventually, towards The Kaims. What are the Kaims? Are they a long wavy earthwork? They are huge banks of pebbles, large and small, covered in short green turf and the height varies between, I'd say, twenty and forty feet higher than the surrounding moorland. [I discovered, looking in the dictionary several weeks later, that "kames" (sic) are ridges or mounds of sand and gravel left by water from melting glaciers]. Whatever their purpose or origin was, they made good walking along their crest for about a mile, after which I followed a fence beside a stream, shown on the map, until a "gate" (wooden, in the shape of a gate but impossible to open) for the track to pass through. After the "gate" there was a standing stone, perhaps a guidepost, but attached to it was some sort of wire cage. What for? However, when the track or path reached the road the stile over the barbed wire fence was broken so I had to try to balance it on its support so that I could climb over without damaging clothing or myself. It was a relief to get over in one piece without mishap.

Across the road was an inviting green track. The wall gave shelter from a cool breeze so I stopped here for lunch before the wall came to an end. As I headed on northward along the track I saw the rich red-brown of a fox nearby, but it was behaving strangely - that jumping about was no courtship display. I had just realised that the poor creature was caught in a snare when a final leap of panic pulled the stake from the ground and the fox was off to freedom, if the stake would give enough freedom for it to survive. The ground showed signs of a long struggle - hunting is a far better method of control; the fox either dies quickly or escapes to live another day, without those hours of struggle and pain and maybe hunger and thirst - had it been there since last night? This was early afternoon. My feelings were of relief at its escape, but for many a day I could see it in my mind, leaping and panting there until it finally broke away.

I thought I should just be able to continue along the track, as shown on the map, until I reached Henlaw Wood and then down to the road, but the track disappeared and no long stretch of woodland came into view so I headed slightly eastward and came down to the road near the previous small woodland. I had already had to backtrack where an electric fence of four wires crossed my route so I must have been considerably delayed by now, not that the time mattered as I wasn't meeting anyone and there was plenty of daylight. Further along the road at Henlaw Wood, which was now in two smaller sections instead of one long wood, there was no sign of any track going up on to the moor where I should have come down. I stopped on the grass verge for a drink of water and a piece of caramel shortbread, feeling quite tired after all my efforts, then revived to continue along the lane to Longformacus and a welcome Southern Upland Way signpost.

All I did at Longformacus was to phone Rose, but she was not available so I left the village at 4.15pm and had pleasant walking up a wooded lane until just before the farm at Rawburn. Up the hill here I was walking against the south-west wind, the higher the windier. The tarmac track descended, still with strong wind, to Watch Water reservoir, where I was nearly blown off my feet as I turned the north-east corner. I pressed on with difficulty, passing sheep and lambs while oystercatchers called, past Scarlaw Farm, then a gate took me on to a sandy, stony track past a strip of old open woodland and on to the open moor. Where the Southern Upland Way was signed to the left I decided to follow it across Watch Water to find a sheltered pitch on its far bank under the hill.

Although there were a few gusts as I pitched, it is quite sheltered. Water was fetched and food soaked then I sat comfortably to enjoy soup, lentils, broccoli and celery in onion and chive sauce with mash, then dehydrated yoghurt with banana slices and crumbled digestive biscuits, then a mug of tea. The new batteries were installed in the radio and the candle lit so now I am listening to Classic FM by cheerful candlelight as I write this. Let's hope for a less windy, less tiring day tomorrow. The wind was the really tiring element today. However, I still got to where I'd planned to be. It was 14 ½ miles but it felt like more.

Thursday 15th April
- Watch Water to Blinkbonny Burn via Lammer Law:

After yesterday's efforts I needed my sleep; from 9.15pm when I settled down I slept until 7.35am, but a later start does not matter, as today is an easier day. The calls of grouse, snipe and curlew accompanied breakfast and packing, then I studied the maps. I walk off Landranger sheet 74 today and on to the Edinburgh map where there are (as Tony Wilson would say) many options. A grassy track, which later became stony, led past grouse butts to Dye Cottage then along beside Dye Water, where I stopped to eat a pear at ten to eleven. There were oystercatchers, a wren and meadow pipits along here. Above, I saw a bird of prey, possibly a hen harrier - dark brown, flying low.

Today's walking was all along these tracks through the Lammermuirs, heather covered hills with the dark brown of heather, green of grass or moss and black of burnt areas - they were burning heather near one of the pylons past Little Law. I think it was about 12 o'clock when I passed a wooden chalet-type building with a boy of eight or nine playing outside. A lady came out and said she'd seen me when she had driven past earlier and would I like a lift to Edinburgh? I explained that I couldn't accept a lift, not that I wanted one anyway, because I was walking from Land's End to John O'Groats. She said, "Well, come back if you change your mind," then I heard her tell her son, "That lady's walking from Land's End to John O'Groats!"

As I continued up the valley, still by Dye Water, a spot or two of rain fell so I decided that an early lunch would be a good idea before any heavier rain came on. I sat with my back and rucksack against a large clump of rushes and tucked into a wholemeal roll with sardine and tomato, then chocolate caramel shortbread, and two fingers of shortbread. The sound of a vehicle approaching along the track made me wonder if it was the lady returning to Edinburgh, but it was a tractor and ahead of it, loping along faster than the tractor, was a blue mountain hare.

A glance at the map showed me the name of a burn just ahead, flowing down from the north - Burn Betwixt Laws! These were Meikle and Little Laws. By the time I reached the pylons and saw the low flames of the heather burners, who were attending to the burning, the rain was falling steadily so I stopped to put on over-trousers. The track, now higher and fairly level, ran westward here but my view through the Gore-Tex hood was mostly of stones, grass, moss, heather and grey clouds. The map shows the track dropping steeply to cross a burn. No buildings are shown but when I looked down during the descent I saw a green shed, then a wooden build-ing, which turned out to be a log cabin shooting hut with a veranda, which reminded me of Anne during a week at Mallaig and "These are my dry socks!" as we sheltered on a veranda and she squeezed out her socks. However, my dry socks were dry, away in the ruck-sack, but a sit on the veranda out of the rain would be welcome. Unfortunately the wind blew straight along it so I sat behind a short log protrusion and my rucksack for a few minutes and nibbled some fruitcake. Even so, it was not very warm so I was soon off again to look for suitable rocks on which to cross the burn below the ford. Another boot print showed that I was not the only one to have walked here.

The steep ascent warmed me up then at the track junction I turned north under Crib Law (509mtrs). Suddenly the sky ahead looked lighter; the rain stopped, and although dark clouds were scudding over the hills to the south they seem to be leaving this area clear. Grouse called "Go-back, go-back," and larks sang. I took a photo of Lammer Law ahead, apparently the highest of the Lam-mermuirs at 527m (1813 feet); the summit cairn would be a good viewpoint and I felt the urge to go up there, but I'd prefer not to wade through deep, wet heather. I would only go up it if a path went that way. I continued along the track until it reached the highest part of the ridge, and then there was a small gate on the left, and a path running along beside the wire fence! There was the print of a walking boot and one of a spiked running shoe! Right - that was just what I wanted, so I proceeded along the path to a track (not shown on the map) and on up left to the cairn. As I walked round the cairn I could see the sea; the sun shone between the clouds and I took a photo of the cairn and trig point, which somebody had crowned with a grouse feeder of pyramid shape, as can be seen in the photo. Below were fields of green and red-brown and the more distant glint of the grey sea of the Firth of Forth. Well, that was certainly an added delight, to be able to go up there on Lammer Law with its wide views, and I didn't want to pitch the tent too early anyway.

I returned to the track, which led quite steeply down, stopping to sit on a bank of convenient height to relieve my knees; the knees don't like long or steep downhill stretches. With binoculars I could see the "building" where I planned to leave the track - it was only a rusty corrugated iron shed and a sheepfold, whichwas made of corrugated iron too. Here on the left was levelish grass that I crossed to reach Blinkbonny Burn, an attractive name but a much tinier burn than I had expected when I had chosen the pitch from the map. There was plenty of time to look for the most level area, which I eventually found beside an almost dead juniper bush. There were a few other junipers here too. Just as I was pitching the rain started, but not seriously until all was under cover and I had fetched lovely clear water from Blinkbonny Burn.

Everything has worked out very well today - the strong wind of yesterday has gone, shelter from the rain at the shooting hut, easy walking over 12 or 12 ½ miles including Lammer Law, a nice scenic green pitch at Blinkbonny Burn and the rain well-timed at the end. Added to that, I saw three golden plover on Lammer Law near the cairn; it was lovely to be so close to them. I am now well-fed but not tired so I'll have a wash now then listen to Classic FM, and to the pleasant gurgles of Blinkbonny Burn and the calls of grouse and curlew before I settle down for the night.

Friday 16th April
- Blinkbonny Burn to Drem:

A cock pheasant gave the alarm call at 6.50 this morning, standing resplendent among the rushes on the far bank of the burn. There was bright blue sky but the sun was not yet over the near hill to the east so it still felt a bit nippy. Breakfast was porridge, boiled egg and my last half slice of toast. As I packed, the sun reached the tent and dried last night's rain. Curlew and grouse called, and the pheasant. At 9.15 I set off back to the track and down towards farmland. A tractor turned into a field of sheep and lambs. Two cyclists came from the other direction, heading for the hills. The track was now a lane, then there was a quiet road into Gifford, where I arrived just after the clock struck eleven. On the previous road I had seen three-cornered leek (or similar), cowslips - one fully out and others in bud - also dog's mercury, celandines and wood anemones.

In Gifford I had to buy some food, a stamp and post off a film. The food was a tin of mackerel fillets for tonight, a carrot and some mash, a tomato, and a Mars bar and banana for my immediate needs, also a packet of sultana scones, 3 for the price of 2, one of which I ate sitting on a seat near the white church with a central tower at the top of the main street. I found a bin for the rubbish and eventually left, still in sunshine, at 11.47am.

There seemed to be no alternative to the B road to Haddington but it was quiet and I could walk along the verge now and then. However, the verge, like many road verges in Scotland, except in the north, was littered with plastic bottles, Irn Bru in particular. Every few yards there was a plastic bottle. I decided that the motorists should see how unsightly they are and began to hit them with a pole as I passed - three tries allowed, before I moved on - so that they landed in the gutter or edge of the road. Why on earth can't people take them home? The car can carry their minimal weight after all.

I stopped in some unfenced woodland to remove a layer, as it was quite warm now, and have a drink of water while a woodpecker knocked on a tree and a wren sang. Time passed quickly; I soon reached the narrow lane for Haddington where I stopped in the shade for my sardine roll and tomato. It was not long before I was walking into Haddington with the sun now gone behind the clouds, then past some old cottages and over the old bridge, where I took a photo then followed the Town Centre signs. It took a while to find what I wanted: two bread rolls, eggs (I had to buy 6 but they are free range, Scottish) and an apple, then as it started to rain I went into a café for a pot of tea and a shortcake sandwich biscuit. It had poured down while I was in there but was brighter as I made my way out of town following the directions of the greengrocer's lady - right at the traffic lights and up to the roundabout. Next a pleasant footpath led below the Garleton Hills to the lane - it would have been nice to camp in those hills but there was no water - then I took a photo of a cow and calf in a field at the farm with a castle ruin beside it. Grey clouds hid the sun; a few spots of rain fell, then more, so the Gore-Tex jacket was required.

I decided to ask about camping soon but the lady at the first place after Camptoun said no, she was sorry, and appeared to be half asleep or half drunk. The man at the next house said he had something in the field so try the farm on the left at Drem. The lady here said she was expecting horses back from an event but gave me some water. I retraced my steps to where a level crossing is shown on the map and had to climb a fence on the other side of the railway then down a grassy track beside a wood until a fallen tree blocked the way. It is quite adequate as a pitch, although traffic is a bit noisy - I prefer the trains. There are also pheasants and wood pigeons. The grid ref is 498792.

The sky over the coast is peach coloured. I'll reach the coast tomorrow, which will be a change of scene. I have had a good meal of fresh carrot, nettles - growing here - and mash with the mackerel fillets - very tasty - and I'll use the oil from them to fry an egg in the morning. Now I'll study the map for tomorrow's route. Today's was 14 miles, or just over.

I had a phone signal tonight so it was good to talk to a few people, but there is not a lot of battery left now and it has to last as far as Edinburgh. I seem to phone one family member, one Backpackers Club member and one friend on average, when I have a signal.

Saturday 17th April
- Drem to Musselburgh, via Aberlady:

It was a bright morning and I'd slept well - what time was it? Only ten to six - had my watch battery given up? I switched on to Classic FM to find, in a few minutes, that it was six o'clock. The sun was just above the horizon shining straight on to the tent, melting frost. There were no sounds yet of trains or traffic, just wood pigeons, a pheasant and a cacophony of gulls. Well, I could take my time and enjoy porridge, fried egg, tea and - luxury today - oatcakes with marmalade! By then the sun was warm, drying tentand towel, then at twenty to nine I was off, over the "level crossing" and fences and walking down the lane signed "Myreton Motor Museum."

Two large leeks lay beside the road just before the museum. Even one of them would be heavy to carry, I thought, and then I saw a smaller one. This, with some of the top leaves removed, would be fine, so it went into a carrier bag. After the next road junction I stopped on the wide verge for a snack and drink of water. A tractor rumbled past with a high trailer behind it - loaded with leeks! So that's where the leeks had come from. Soon after this a greenfinch landed on the hedge just in front of me, then flew on a few yards. Two or three cowslips were just opening on the grass verge. I went on to Aberlady where I bought some chocolate chip biscuits and a brown roll - they didn't sell a lot of food at the PO there - then I walked down to the estuary of the Peffer Burn and Aberlady Bay.

At first a tarmac track led to the golf club then a grassy path followed round the coast - delightful walking in sunshine with occasional buds of thrift opening, the rocky shore below and views over blue water to the misty hills to the north. From Craigielaw Point the beach was walkable, at first over a bank of mussel shells, then small cockleshells and the odd razor shell, until it climbed to a grassy point at the end of the Nature Reserve (No erecting of tents etc, said a sign here) near the hotel. From here the path ran between the wall and the beach but must have been washed away at some point so I turned back and had to cut through the hotel garden - if it was still a hotel - there was no sign at the end of the drive that I could see, but a pathway crossed the drive before the road so I turned right along it, through woodland then coastal grassland as the path continued past where I'd previously reached, by the wall. I even saw two or three violets here, and daisies and dandelions.

While crossing a car park I saw a sign "John Muir Way" so took a photo, which turned out to be the last one today. There was a small white flower, quite a lot of them, very similar to chickweed but almost enclosed by a leaf - I must look it up. (After I got home I found that it was Montia Perfoliata - my book gave no English name). The breeze was quite chilly from the west, especially on Ferny Point, but further on a sunny, sheltered hollow provided a warm spot for a lunch consisting of a "real bread" crusty roll with half the smoked cheese, a bit of raw leek and wild greens of chickweed and garlic mustard followed by a scone - I'd eaten my Grasmere gingerbread and apple earlier. I relaxed in the sunshine here from one o'clock to half past then walked on again. At about 1.45 at Longniddry I saw the campsite that I'd originally planned to use, before I'd divided one long day into two shorter ones. "Seton Sands Holiday Park" announced the sign, and I noted that the tents were alongside the road so would suffer from traffic noise. Although I didn't want to camp, I thought I would enquire about the price while I was passing and popped into reception.

"How much would it be for one small backpacking tent?"

"Depending on the season - now it is £13."

"That's a lot for one person."

"Well, that includes four people."

"But I'm only one person!"

"It includes all facilities. Would you like a brochure?"

"Not at that price, thank you."

Thank goodness there is another site shown on map before Musselburgh!

The John Muir Way went on, sometimes as now, on the road or on a concrete walkway next to the beach, or a tarmac path over a headland. While on the road at Prestonpans I bought some milk and chocolate at a shop there - it's a pity there were no vegetables or fruit. More than a few spots of rain began to fall so the Gore-Tex jacket went on then the industrial museum was in sight, which meant that I should turn left here for the campsite, Drum Mohr. A pleasant lady welcomed me, asked me to fill in a card then said she thought £5 for one walker - what a difference! There is a £2 deposit for a toilet/shower block key. She also kindly said that I could pitch on the lawn behind the house, which would be quiet for me; it is also sheltered from the wind, which I can hear in the trees above. I cooked a meal of soup, dehydrated roast beef with celery and carrots and half the leek that I'd found, rice, and garlic and herb sauce, then chocolate semolina and tea. I phoned Dad, Lynette and Dave & Liz Lee at Witcombe to report on my progress, before going to wash up, then I had a lovely hot shower.

Now I have lit the candle. The wind is still rushing through the trees and the rain is pattering on the tent. I have looked at the map and the little free guide map of Edinburgh and feel excited at being only a few miles away - Edinburgh, that distant place, is close and I have walked here! Today was 11½, or 12 miles with the extra bit. I expect to use a YHA hostel tomorrow in the city centre. I haven't mentioned the eider ducks, certainly one of the delights of the day - I saw a small group at Seton Harbour and loved hearing their oooh-oooh-ooooh!

Sunday 18th April
- Musselburgh to Edinburgh: (about 10 miles today):

Heavy rain was falling at ten to seven so the thick socks that I'd left on the line would be even wetter. I went to wash my hair about 7.30 so that it would finish drying while I had breakfast, after a rub with the towel and two or three minutes under the hot air of the hand-drier. The rain had just stopped when I was ready to move so I packed a wet flysheet. I did not get away very early due to talking to the nice lady at reception, so it was eventually ten past ten. She gave me a site sticker, a postcard of the site (15p), a Scottish Camp-sites leaflet, labelled 75p, and some leaflets about Drum Mohr so the map case is loaded!

Down the lane a coaltit flew on to a small tree near me, then I crossed the main road to join the John Muir Way again. This goes past the lagoons, which are out of sight from the track so you don't see them unless you go to the bird hide. I didn't go, but the birds on the beach and water were mute swans, golden eye, curlew, oyster-catchers, and a dunlin. The Way curved southward beside the River Esk to the first bridge then on to Fisherrow harbour, where I took a photo and read the information board telling of the days when it was a fishing port.

Joppa was reached by road; a sign read: "Welcome to Porto-bello and Joppa, Edinburgh's Seaside." There were some seaside gardens but no seats to sit to enjoy them; the next seats faced the road, not the sea! Who would want to sit looking at traffic when the sea was nearby, over the wall? Portobello began with palatial PCs and a bandstand/shelter type building with seats all facing outward around it. The rain had stopped now and I had the pleasure of a walk along a sandy beach for a mile. The tide was going out leaving lacy patterns of coal dust and a dark tide line. There was lots of golden sand and many shells. The sands were used by a few dog walkers and runners and one or two family groups. I left after the final groyne to have my lunch on a seat on the promenade. It was only 12.30 but I did not suppose that I'd be able to sit down during the three-mile walk to Waverley Station.

This road walk into Edinburgh was soon over. I was going home for three days to get the Backpack journal pages filled then off to the printers. Here at Waverley I collected my train tickets from the Fast Ticket machine, the first time I'd used one, then I browsed around the Tourist Information Centre but it was too hot in there to stay for long so I went to somewhere on the station that gave infor-mation on accommodation to find the address of the SYHA hostel. Lots of people were sitting in the sunshine in Waverley Gardens. I walked along Princes Street and neighbouring streets wondering if there were any tempting tea rooms but did not see any.

After getting my tickets and enquiring about the hostel I'd crossed Princes Street to Waterstones book shop to get an Explorer map of Edinburgh, including the Forth Bridge, then I can walk that way tomorrow and get a bus or train back to Waverley Station, I hope. I eventually turned left on to Palmerston Place, passing a large Church of Scotland (service 6.30pm) and Cathedral (service 3pm) before turning second left on to Eglinton Crescent for the hostel. It is £13 for the night, in room 26, which is up lots of stairs on the top floor, I think, so it is useful to have fit legs!

I had time to dig out my food bag from the bottom of the rucksack, go down to the members' kitchen in the basement, make two mugs of tea and cook couscous with leek, mash and a hard-boiled egg, followed by dehydrated banana and peach slices with crumbled digestive biscuits and custard. After washing up I had time for a shower before leaving for church, the one I'd passed on the way here, at 6.18pm. I was welcomed by the assistant minister, James Thornton, enjoyed the service - well-known hymns and a well-thought-out sermon by a lady. I think the four young ladies sitting in front of me were also visitors. Now back at the hostel I can't be bothered to go up all those stairs again yet so I'm sitting in the Ballantyne room at the front of the house to write my diary and look at maps. Earlier there had been several Thai or Chinese youngsters chatting away as they prepared their food in the kitchen.

Again, it is exciting to have reached this landmark in the journey and I look forward to adding a few more miles towards the Forth Railway Bridge tomorrow, then continuing northward on Friday. I must get back to the maps now!

Monday 19ᵗʰ April
- Edinburgh to Forth Railway Bridge and Dalmeny Station:
9½ miles today.

A note in the fridge told members to use up the food left by those who had gone, which was all on one shelf, dated of course. I helped myself to a couple of small rashers of bacon to have with my egg.

From the Youth Hostel I made my way to an old railway walk/cycleway, followed it for some way and ended up at a roundabout, then turned left along Ferry Road and the next road on the right took me down past some shops, where I bought a roll and a chocolate éclair at Gregg's bakers, before continuing down to the coast. It was cloudy and tried to rain a bit, but I was pleased to see a path leading down through the trees from Marine Drive to the shore, where there was a wide promenade between the grass and the sea wall. When I reached the River Almond I looked for the ferry; a blue notice board said that the ferry was for foot passengers only, 50p each, and that it did not run if the river was in spate. I stood looking at it. Was it in spate? Well, perhaps - it did look to be quite a rapid current so I went along to the café to ask, as I could see no boat. "The ferry has not run for four years," the lady said. Oh. That meant going up the River Almond Walkway, which was actually very pleasant, beside the river under trees. The rain had stopped and there was blue sky now. Three-cornered leek and ramsons grew there; there were craggy cliffs on the far side and trees with their spring buds opening. Steps took me up over a rocky section, and down again.

The path led to Cramond Old Bridge but it was cycleway from then on alongside the road - noisy where it was the A90 but quieter where the A90 left and the B road continued. This walking beside roads was disappointing after the expectation of a woodland coastal walk on the Dalmeny Estate. I turned off for Dalmeny Station to check the train times for my return to Edinburgh: 14.50, 14.58 and 15.20pm, any of which would be in time for my 3.50pm train to Crewe. Now I continued down another railway/cycleway between trees with occasional glimpses of the Forth Railway Bridge crossing the Firth of Forth - I've been over a few times by train but not seen it like this before, so this was another exciting landmark on my route. The way took me to South Queensferry then I returned to Dalmeny in time for the 2.50pm train to Waverley - and was actually home by 7.50pm - 5 hours all the way! There was a pile of post to be opened of course, then next day e-mails and washing to deal with, and on Wednesday I took Dad shopping and filled some more pages of Backpack, managing to get it to the printers on Thursday after many hours on the computer, then the evening was occupied with mowing the back lawn and packing. (My kind neighbours had mowed the front lawn). It will be good to be walking again after all this!

Friday 23rd May 2004
- Dalmeny Station to Fordel Firs:
What a hectic three days! The walking is so easy and relaxing compared with all that rushing around to get a lot done in a short time.

There was no five-hour journey this time. I left home at 9.25 to get an early bus in case the next one ran late and missed the train but, of course, the train was about ¾ hour late arriving at Crewe. A rather indistinct announcement on the train told us that we could have a free drink of tea or coffee if we went to the buffet car so I went for tea later in the journey. Passengers wanting Edinburgh were also told to change at Carlisle, which meant another 50 minutes or so to wait, then we reached Edinburgh around 3.30pm. I dashed off for a ticket to Dalmeny (£1.90) and found platform 18 for the hot and crowded train. Some windows were open but the heat must have been on, so I was very glad to get out into the fresh air at four o'clock.

It felt strange to be walking through a housing estate following Cycle Route 1, which goes over the Forth Road Bridge. Cyclists and walkers have their own separate section of bridge. The traffic produced so much vibration that I only took one photo; it was cloudy anyway. There were good views of the Forth Railway Bridge of course, and of boats moored at North Queensferry. You come off the bridge next to gorse bushes in a rocky cutting before the road/cycleway leaves for Inverkeithing. Bryan Crick had suggested doing as they did, using the B981 to Fordell Firs Scout Headquarters. The road walking was relieved by grass verges now and then.

There was nobody around at Reception so I found someone to ask about camping - he told me where the Warden was, up the field, so I went to enquire - it seemed that one had to be a member of the Scout Association to camp there, but I mentioned that I used to help with the Cubs and that I'd been a Guide, so I was allowed to camp - "You're very welcome," he said. I pitched the tent near some trees away from groups of scouts and cubs, for peace, and near a tap - but no water came out so I had to look elsewhere. I am tired after a couple of late nights so I don't think the Scouts' and Cubs' excited noise will disturb me! I phoned Anne before settling down then I was soon asleep.

Today was only 5½ miles, since 4pm of course, all hard surface except for a bit of grass verge here and there beside the road. Tomorrow will be a refreshing change with coastal walking for most of the day.

Saturday 24th April
- Fordel Firs to Dunnikier, Kirkcaldy, via Aberdour:
The night was surprisingly peaceful; I slept well until traffic noise woke me then soon a robin was singing in a bush nearby. I went for

a shower and in the washroom I was shocked to see soap wrappers and a toothpaste carton lying around - there is a bin - and water left in a basin. I binned those items then had a shower and breakfast. As I walked up the track or drive at nine o'clock I realised that I hadn't taken a photo so I took one of the attractive wooden Fordell Firs Welcome sign at the entrance. After 2½ miles of road walking, mostly between fields and woods, I reached the Fife Coast Path. It was good to see the path sign and to walk between the trees with views of Dalgety Bay. I phoned Dad, who said there was blue sky and sunshine at Sandbach, whereas it is cloudy but warm here.

Pleasant coastal walking took me to the ruins of St Bridget's Church, which dates from the twelfth century onward. I stopped to look around and took a photo from the wall above the beach - the furthest away that I could manage; another step backwards would have landed me on the beach. Rucksack on again, I returned to the path, which left the coast to continue along a tarmac track lined with daffodils, where there was a tree stump with a plank nailed on it for a seat. I sat here to eat a Satsuma then I phoned Sue at Dunollie to enquire about last year's food parcel and tell her when I expected to reach Aberfeldy. After taking care of it for a year, Sue will kindly take it to the campsite by Wednesday, when I'm due to arrive there. The campsite had not been open when I sent the parcel so I had obtained the Dunollie address from a library book.

At Aberdour the path led to the main village street before heading coastward again down a lane, but on this street was a church with a Coffee Morning poster outside. I'd just been wondering if there was a café for a pot of tea. For £1 I had a slice of cherry cake, a scone and 2½ cups of tea. Several friendly people spoke to me, asked about the walk and what charities I was raising money for, and gave me a total of £13 for these. I took a photo of the "tea and cake" ladies then, refreshed and refuelled, I went down the lane to the coast and little harbour (I changed a film on a seat overlooking the harbour), then the path climbs steep steps up the hillside on to the cliff top, where birds twittered unseen in thick gorse, before the descent to Silver Bay, where I stopped on the level grassy sea front for my cheese roll. I'd just seen a greenfinch and robin as I reached the level grass near the sea.

The Fife Coast Path continued between the railway and the sea, quite attractive, with the sun shining now. At Burntisland I posted the Aberdour card to Julia, and sent off the film I'd finished.

Between Burntisland and Kinghorn, was a stone monument in memory of King Alexander III, the last Celtic king of Scotland, who died here in an accident. I wondered what the accident was; a man who was reading it said that the king's horse stumbled on the edge of the hill above and he fell to his death. There was great sadness throughout the land, no feasting or any sign of joy. Sad.

From Kinghorn to Kirkcaldy was a lovely stretch of coast path with views - hazily to Musselburgh - and along the path grew gorse, violets, daisies, a few bluebells and, best of all, some cowslips. I took a photo of some. The ruined Seafield Tower stood beside the sea here but there was no information board to tell of its history. The town was not worth a photo as I approached it, due to being spoilt by high blocks of flats near the front. I walked along the beach for the last half mile or so to Kirkcaldy, then found that I had to wade through a stream to reach the main beach - I'd tried a path above the beach which led to a brick wall but there was too big a drop on the other side - anyway, the stream did not go over my boots tops. There was now a mile or so of promenade before I crossed the road for another mile's walk past the hospital to Dunnikier Caravan Park (campsite, actually).

I was relieved to arrive and get the tent pitched on the grass under the trees, with one other tent, being tired after road walking and carrying a heavy rucksack on a hot day, although only the last couple of road miles since leaving the beach were tiring. A shower was welcome while the food was soaking. I washed both pairs of socks then enjoyed a mug of tea, macaroni cheese with cauliflower and leek, then apple and peach slices with custard. I phoned Katie before writing my diary. I am now dropping asleep after a lovely coastal day. I had enjoyed watching three curlews wading nearby while I was having lunch, and a group of eider ducks "oo-oooh-ing"

Ooooh! Lovely. 15½ miles.

Sunday 25th April 2004
- Kirkcaldy to wild on East Lomond, via Thornton:
I was very tired last night, settled down just before ten o'clock, and was soon asleep. Unfortunately, traffic noise woke me at 2.30am and I was still awake at 3.40. I listened to the owls. Of course, I next woke up late at 7.55am so went and washed my hair so that it would dry while I had my breakfast of muesli, boiled egg and toast (one

year old toast!) Everything was packed by 9.45am then I went to return the toilet/shower key and get the LEJOG form signed. I asked if there was a way out at the top of the wood, to be told to go along the hotel drive, past the hotel then turn right at the end. I passed the hotel and looked at the map. The route suggested seemed a long way round, and what when I reached the A92? The lady had not known if you could go across the fields to the river. I decided to retrace my steps from the hotel and try the woodland paths to see if there was a way out to the north. At least my left knee was not twinging or aching today, as it was yesterday afternoon (I was using only one pole then); it felt better for a rest overnight.

A lovely patch of wood sorrel called for a photo. The woodland paths were delightful, even though they didn't go where I wanted to go, to a northerly exit, so I looped back round to the campsite path. I was just thinking, "What a waste of an hour," when I reminded myself that it was not at all; I had really enjoyed that woodland walk, even if it was not progress in my chosen direction - I'm glad I did those two miles; they were a bonus. Now I returned to my original idea of walking up the industrial estate road, with a track shown at the end and, joy! There was a sign for the cycleway and a public footpath sign to Thornton. This was good. A straight path ran between grass and gorse and other bushes, then reached a footbridge over the A92, after which the cycleway went to the right and the footpath straight on, again grassy with hoof prints on it. Later three horses and riders passed the other way, then as I sat on the river bridge to eat an apple a lady with two dogs passed me. It was really warm now.

The path took me to Thornton where I bought some Kingsmill Malted Wheat bread for my next three days' lunches, and a cherry yoghurt, which I had later on the grass verge sheltered by a broom bush. Further on, in a field to the right, a young dark bay horse pranced about, interested to see me but uncertain of my "strange" appearance with pack on back.

The woodside path shown on the map at Eastfield was now beside an industrial estate road (new since the map was printed) where, at a bus stop, a little girl about four years old came to up me saying, "Look! On my hand - a ladybird!"

I found a way into the woodland for lunch, to remove my boots and relax in comfort, although there was a lot of litter there. Onward now, through the industrial estate with its nice wide grass verges to walk on, until I came to the "yellow road" near Glenrothes. I asked a lady about crossing the A92 further on and she said there was a flyover. This took me to a footpath/cycleway beside the road and later the cycleway turned off left to Cadham, just right. Along the Cadham road, lovely and quiet, I sat on a grassy bank under a tree for a drink of water and phoned Anne Marshall. When I'd walked on for half a mile I realised that I'd left my glasses on the bank so rushed back - Yes, they were still there.

The next section of road had wide grass verges - I had a sit down after my rushing back - and I kept to the shady side of the road where possible as it was quite warm by now. At last I came to Pitcairn where a path, unsigned, left the road in the right place, for I was heading for the Lomond Hills, East and West Lomond, which are not high but are the highest land in the area. This was the sort of walking I wanted - away from roads - a gate into the forest, a path up beside the forest, a drop to cross the Coal Burn, up beside more forest, then beside a field of cows and calves to more mature, darker forest, then out on to a track and there was the stream shown on the map, a tiny one but clear and running, so I filled the water bottles then took a photo of a large clump of primroses before going through a gate in the deer fence. Pausing for breath, I turned to take a photo looking back to the coast. Now that I had water I had freedom so I could choose my pitch. Here, on soft grass beneath scattered trees? Open hillside? No, I'd like to go further. Steps led to the parking area with seats - I was ready for a seat after carrying water up there, and sat to enjoy the view. A couple came along and asked about the walk and tried my rucksack - heavy! - so I took out the water bottles and they found it much better! After a short rest I went on up the East Lomond path, the sun in my eyes, onward, upward, with a pause for breath and to look at the view, a few people overtaking me.

A kestrel hovered, and another one; a bumblebee buzzed about. Earlier there had been red admiral and peacock butterflies on this lovely sunny day. Now there was a last steep bit, some rock, grass again, then the view indicator on the levelish green summit. I wandered around the top - should I pitch up here or lower down? After looking at and considering lower down, up here at 424 metres would be very pleasant on a sunny evening, so I chose a spot about 15 yards west and slightly below the top. The tent was soon pitched, and the food put to soak - turkey, celery, carrot and red pepper, rice and garlic sauce - delicious! A mug of tea came first then apple and peach crumble and custard after.

At nine o'clock I looked out to see a colourful sunset glow so I nipped out with the camera. How lovely to be up there alone in this peaceful, high spot, quiet with no traffic sounds, with the rich sunset colours, a view along the ridge to the dark shape of West Lomond, and a gentle breeze. An outstanding end to the day and tomorrow will start with a lovely ridge walk along to West Lomond.

Monday 20th April
- East Lomond and West Lomond to Bridge of Earn:

How lovely to wake to the sun shining on the tent and to unzip to a marvellous view, the hills clear but mist still over the Firth of Forth. Breakfast was porridge, baked beans, bread and tea then I put the remaining cheese and lettuce between slices of bread for lunch. I took a photo of the tent in this marvellous setting, finished packing then set off at twenty five past nine. I was sorry to leave here but West Lomond at 522 metres looked enticing at the end of the ridge. First the path descended steeply from East Lomond then there was easy level walking along a grassy track. Beside the track at one point were some fully open wood anemones - the spring flowers continue to give pleasure. The track dropped to an almost empty car park and toilets, then another track led gently upwards towards West Lomond. Where a small burn crossed the track I stopped for a good mugful of fresh cool water, the only water along here, then on to where a sign pointed right "to avoid erosion." Round the side of the hill a path led steeply upward so, after fifty yards or so, I left the rucksack on a level shelf not far from the path and romped up more easily. Again, there were wide views all round but it was hazy in the distance. After a summit photo I stepped up to the base of the trig pillar to be sure that I'd really been to the top, then I walked easily down to the waiting rucksack.

The track now ascended slightly then Loch Leven came into view. That's odd; the track should have descended, but there is a narrow path heading straight down. It led to a wire fence and a very steep drop, which was obviously not the way and meant heading back to the grassy track and looking for a way heading off it in the right direction. I found it - not very obvious, but there was a narrow green path which soon dropped steeply, down, down, down over the close contour lines, then it followed a fence and went less steeply to the remains of a stone wall. I sat down to give my knees some relief and thought I might as well have a longer break and an early lunch. An interesting rock formation in the sheep pasture a little below to my left was not marked on the map but, I discovered at the next gateway, that the rocks were the Bonnet Stones - their origin not known.

Now quiet lanes took me to Gateside, where a pub on the corner was useful for a glass of pineapple juice with ice in to refresh me; the only occupants, the barman and the landlord, each donated £3 for the Walk. After talking for a while I refilled a water bottle and set off again in warm sunshine. The next mile and a bit on the A912 passed quickly with very little traffic, then a lane to the left climbed to Old Fargie then wound downhill to Conland Farm where a lady on a horse came out leading another grey horse. In a few minutes I was over the motorway bridge and stopped on the grass verge for a drink of water and piece of flapjack with boots and socks off for a ten-minute break. With "new feet" I crossed the B road to another quiet lane to Fordel and Lochelbank. I was relieved to see a foot-path sign where the farm track left the road.

When I reached the farm I asked the farmer, who showed me where to leave the farmyard, about the route to Dron Hill and he told me to follow "the road" (track) to a gate that may or may not be open, then look for a ruin on the hill to the right and head for it, after some "hen manure" (spoken in a broad Scots accent). From the gate at the end of the track I couldn't see a ruin so waited for the tractor driver who was working his way up and down the field, and asked him. He pointed to the ruin on the hillside and I saw it now - much smaller and lower than I had expected, more like rocks than the remains of a building, unless you know. Beyond the ruin an old iron gateway had a sign saying that this farm had had a roof on until 1933 and a fine avenue of trees, of which only a few ashes remained after Dutch Elm disease had claimed the elms. It also said that this was the Wallace Road; Sir William Wallace had it constructed for his army and it was used until it was superceded by the present road.

As I walked this route larks had been singing and curlews calling, with blackbirds and wrens in the wooded areas, and a few wheatears in the Lomond Hills. Butterflies again were mostly pea-cocks and a couple of red admirals. The Wallace Road came down to West Don then a green track signed "Bridge of Earn" led for about a mile to another lane where, instead of turning right for Bridge of Earn, I turned left to look for a farm. In a few minutes there was a kissing gate with the sign "Silver Walk." This was a level pathway between trees, including some Scots pines and birches, taking me for a pleasant half mile to a lane where I decided to ask about camping at the second house, which had some stables and therefore probably a field.

Yes, I was made very welcome and while pitching on the lawn in front of the stables (their daughter was the horse owner); I was brought a pot of tea by the kind lady here. When I returned the tray she asked if there was anything else at that I needed. "Well, just one egg for the morning, if you have one to spare." She gave me two, not accepting my offer of payment. Just before this a young lady came along with a black and white Border Collie, returning it to its owner after walking it. This was Misty, the dog and young lady I'd seen earlier along the Silver Walk!

Now I have just tucked into dehydrated liver and onions, swede, broccoli and mash, with added fresh carrot found by the roadside this afternoon, then chocolate dessert. I have phoned Bryan Crick, who has had the misfortune to break his collar bone on a bus that stopped suddenly, and Rose, who does not think she can afford the train fare to join me at Lairg, later in the walk. After going to the house for a wash and cleaning my teeth I'm ready to settle down for the night. The flowers seen today were: three-cornered-leek, primroses, violets, celandines, stitchwort, water avens, and the chickweed-type flower which appears to be Montia perfoliata, the flower I had first seen on the John Muir Way.

Tuesday 27th April 2004
- Bridge of Earn via Dupplin Castle to Harrietfield:

I think it rained nearly all night but I slept well then went in for a wash in the morning. I had almost finished packing by 9 o'clock when the good lady appeared and asked if there was anything I needed, as she was just taking Misty for a walk. I thanked her - there was nothing; I just had to pack the flysheet then I was off in waterproofs at ten past nine for the mile to Bridge of Earn. Here was a useful little shop where I bought a Mars bar and a yoghurt for the morning's snacks - it called itself yoghurt but tasted nothing like it; I'd have called it sloppy milk jelly. A mile of A912 led to the little lane for Bryan's recommended route (they used it last year, he said) via Dupplin Castle. By now the sun was shining so I quickly removed the waterproofs before continuing for three miles up the lane along Strath Earn to Aberdalgie, then on past some private entrances to Dupplin Castle, then finally the track to Bankhead. It felt better to be going north again from Bankhead Farm after all those miles west. If I had walked the way I'd planned I should have gone north via Perth, following the river before heading NW on lanes, but this route had a lot of built up area through Perth so, although Bryan's route was longer it was more scenic, probably, and had a variety of wild flowers: Bluebells, celandines, red campion, garlic mustard, chickweed wintergreen (pink), and daisies and dandelions too of course. Today's birds were a couple of buzzards, lapwings, curlew, rooks and crows, wrens, a song thrush, a yellowhammer and blackbirds. After Bankhead and an area of woodland was a T-junction where I sat under a beech tree for my tuna and tomato sandwiches and fruitcake. (8½ to 9 miles here).

To reach Windyedge I had to climb a gate, detour round a pheasant pen, climb another gate, get through a barbed wire fence (Did Bryan go that way?) then all was easy to the road, which had a subway under it. I'd taken a photo of a horse with a Shetland pony on the Dupplin estate, but that was all - I'd been concentrating on getting on.

The lane/road took me to Tibbermore then, before the A85, a track went off to the left for Kinnon Park (farm), which made a nice change from the road. After Kinnon Park, having turned right here, the track became grassy and sloped uphill. I was ready for a break here and sat on the track to take a photo looking back to Kinnon Park, stone buildings among trees, then continued up the short hill where trees now grew beside the track. There were a few spots of rain as I neared Methven. "It won't be much," I thought hopefully, then suddenly it came lashing down, so waterproofs were needed and pulled on as quickly as possible. In the village there may be shelter in a pub or shop - was there a shop? Yes, there was - Spar. In I went and bought a carrot, a pear, a lemon cake and milk, and came out to find the rain almost stopped.

It was 2½ miles to South Arditte, Bryan's and Ron's pitch in this area. Bryan had thought that I'd want to go further and he was right. Just before this I'd stopped for a drink of milk and some lemon cake. The sun was shining and it was too early to stop so I pressed on to Millhaugh where there was a lovely old arched bridge, no longer in use, and I took a photo from the newer bridge now in use. Next came the B8063, a quiet road where I hoped to find the track leading to Glen Shee for a wild pitch. No track visible - fields with barbed wire fences - so where to camp? I went back a little way to Laverock Bank, the previous farm. "No, sorry, the land belongs to the farm up there, Kindrumpark - you'd have to ask there." That was a good mile up hill, and another mile back, so instead I walked on and tried the pub at Harrietfield, set back from the road with a good sized beer garden. The Drumtochty Tavern. "Yes, that should be all right" said the barman, and offered to put the kettle on for some hot water and tea while I pitched. We had a chat about the walk. Back in the tent I enjoyed a couple of mugs of tea while the fresh carrot and couscous were cooking with de-hydrated chicken and I had mushroom and garlic soup with it too, then that was followed with chocolate dessert made with the fresh milk then another slice of lemon cake, which was rather crumbly. A curlew called and the rain pattered down steadily once more.

Now the urgent thing was to look at the map since my chosen track seemed out of the question, being invisible on the ground. The barman had said it was possible to walk over the moors to Amulree. I had written on the map at Amulree, TEA ROOMS? - the information having been obtained from a library book, and tearooms are always good for re-fuelling. If I get off by 8.30am I should get there at lunchtime then, I hope, the weather will allow some good views. There is no mobile phone signal at Harrietfield. Now it is 9.50pm and a curlew is still calling. I'd better settle down now - I'm tired after 17 or 17 ½ miles, but I feel that I've gone well all day.

Wednesday 28th April 2004
- Harrietfield to Aberfeldy, via Amulree:

What a beautiful sunny morning! The birds were in full voice, espe-cially a wood pigeon, and it was unusual to hear a curlew combined with the garden birds! A blackbird made frequent flutterings to and from the hedge so I expect she has a nest there. She also perched on the tent, leaving a white spot, and on the seat by the picnic table. I was on my way by 8.35am. Along the lane a boy sitting under a tree said, "Hiyah!" looking up from his lunchbox; no doubt he was wait-ing for his school bus. A few minutes later a minibus came along. At the sharp bend I turned right to walk up the track. Ahead of me were tall Scots pines against a blue sky, then spring green larches and spring green grass beneath my feet.

A notice on a gate warned me of danger at the disused quarry and to keep to the track, which I did of course, progressing steadily uphill in sunshine with a gentle refreshing breeze. On up, through and past the quarry region, then down between dark but sunny heather covered hills and west along the glen towards Amulree. This was really lovely. I was feeling hungry at 11.30, after breakfast at seven, so stopped for one sandwich, a shortbread finger and the pear. At the highest point of the path there was suddenly a view of Amulree, white houses and green fields with the blue loch beyond. It was so near but so far; it took two hours to reach it, but two really enjoyable hours. The tearoom *was* there so I had a pot of tea and a slice of carrot cake at a table outside looking back up the glen down which I had just walked. That was most enjoyable, both the refreshments and the view.

I left at twenty past one, full of energy, to stride along the road to the track that rises by Deane Haugh Farm, pausing part way up for my other two sandwiches, sitting in warm sunshine with boots off beside a rock. Time to move on - and upward I went, but now, I discovered, the track goes to a radio or phone mast so I was too high up. Rather than drop down the way I had come, I followed the wall to a new forest fence then down beside it, finding a dead deer, which looked as though it had crashed into the fence not knowing that it was there. As I descended carefully some heavy drops of rain fell, though not for long, then I continued in the right direction over rough tussocky ground, which meant very slow going, and there was another forest fence ahead, so I thought the best course of action would be to cross the burn below and get to the road for the walk to Aberfeldy. I made for the Cochill Burn, removed my boots and socks and put on sandals to wade refreshingly across, dried my feet and re-booted, then walked diagonally over to the road. Cool refreshed feet were just what I needed for miles of road walking - I didn't look at my watch but just walked on and was glad when the road at last began to descend. I don't remember any birds except meadow pipits along this road; a lot of the land alongside was forest with one or two open areas. Schiehallion was now in sight and Beinn a'Ghlo, which was nice. Downward and onward.

At last a welcome sign said, "Campsite, 1¼ miles through Town Centre." I thought, "I hoped that it might be nearer, but I'll get there." I did - to a welcome and the food parcel. The tent was pitched and water fetched, then while the food was soaking, I went for a shower and to wash my socks. Then I was ready to tuck into a good meal while oystercatchers called from the River Tay not far off. I was clean, comfortable and well-fed. I phoned Dad, Barbara and Lynette; I don't know where next I'll get a phone signal. I am late writing the diary tonight, doing it by light of the head-torch, but that's after 20 miles of walking. I was too late for the shops, which are not far from the campsite, but I do know what's here: bakers, Co-op, greengrocer only a few minutes' walk away, so I can go in the morning. It's been a lovely day - now for sleep at 10.25pm.

Thursday 29th April
- Aberfeldy to Pitlochry and very wild, windy pitch below Ben Vrachie:

This was a nice, quiet campsite so I slept well. Even the traffic was quiet after ten o'clock. Mine is the only tent in the spacious tent area. After breakfast I walked into the town in sandals, leaving the tent pitched, to buy rolls, Arran Dunlop cheese, Fairtrade chocolate, eggs, apple and banana, a Swiss finger to eat immediately and a scone for tomorrow. Back at the tent I tucked into the banana and tasted a bit of the cheese as a few drops of rain hit the flysheet, and I put some cheese and tomato in a roll for lunch.

After talking to the campsite people and asking if the path to Pitlochry was actually walkable ("Yes, there's a sign at the bottom.") I set off latish - I think it must have been after half past ten. The first part was road for just over four miles to Grandtully, and across the bridge over the River Tay, then a right fork leads to another road almost opposite the footpath sign. The path sloped up beside the golf course, with birch trees and gorse and, higher up, beeches with their new green leaves. I climbed on to the bank by the wall to get a photo, waiting for a cloud to uncover the sun, then continued to where **Cross** is shown on the map. Above the track to my left beneath a tree was a rectangular stone set vertically in the ground with a cross, engraved on one side in outline. I wonder why it is there and how old it is. I climbed back down to sit beside the bank for my lunch, sitting in the sun near Tullypowrie Burn, which the path crossed later.

The path gradually ascended an open hillside of gorse, grass and small trees with streamlets wandering here and there, until the well-used path entered the forest over a stile. In the forest the path was well marked with signs to Strathtay and Pitlochry. The forest track led to a grassy path, which descended between the trees, eventually giving a view over Pitlochry to Ben Vrachie. There was a track once more, then I continued across a lane to a foot suspension bridge opened on 24th May 1913 (there was previously a ferry here). I went under the bridge to take a photo standing at the edge of the river on the stones; from there it was only a few minutes' walk into Pitlochry.

Here I bought and wrote a card to Ken Pickering, looked around the Tourist Information Centre but saw nothing I wanted, bought some stamps at the Post Office and posted Ken's card and the film I'd just finished at the suspension bridge. It was cooler by now so, as I headed up the road towards Moulin, I stopped to put on my Gore-Tex jacket, and later on woolly hat and gloves were required! Near where you change from lane to footpath I changed to the Blair Atholl map - another step forward, and on to a well-used map that has been with me on a few explorations of the Blair Atholl and Glen Tilt area. I met, coming down the path, a lady who stopped to tell me what lovely weather she'd had this week and to ask about my walk. I went on up through the forest to the heathery hillside in a strengthening easterly wind. The path was easy walking, recently restored, a notice said. I watched the clouds sail westward in the wind; there was still blue sky to the east but it was darker to the west. The path turned beside a high craggy bit (photo here) for the final walk to the lochan and the foot of Ben Vrachie.

The question was, where could I pitch out of the wind? A high rock in a corner had short turf near it so I left the rucksack here while I went for water then I tried to pitch. Most of the pegs were in when a strong gust came round behind the rock, flattened the tent and bent the pole. I didn't want that in the night! One peg was missing; I searched for about ten minutes without finding it - perhaps it was flipped into the heather - then I packed up and came down to the slightly boggy area below the path on the bank above. I was nearly blown off my feet on the path. At least it is sheltered down here from the fierce strong gusts even if the ground is uneven and a slightly squelchy, but not too wet. My trouser knees were damp from kneeling to control the tent in the wind so I changed and got into the sleeping bag. I was hungry and ready for my meal of mushroom and garlic soup, lamb with rosemary, carrots and celery with mash, banana custard, tea then a chocolate drink later in the evening as I wrote my diary. I hope it will be a peaceful night then a calmer morning to go up Ben Vrachie - it would have been much too windy this evening. Another enjoyable day - the flowers were wood anemones, wood sorrel, violets and cuckoo flowers. 12 miles today from Aberfeldy.

Friday 30th April 2004
- Below Ben Vrachie via Blair Atholl to Glen Tilt, below Beinn a'Ghlo:

It was a peaceful night below the bank, until the wind woke me at 6 o'clock, battering the tent from the other side. No pegs came out but the wind was driving a pole end into the soft ground so I had less headroom and the inner became unhooked at each gust. Plan: get dressed quickly, have a drink of water and eat muesli - lighting the stove would not be a good idea with the inner becoming un-hooked every few minutes - pack, set off and find a nice sheltered spot somewhere to get the stove out for a good, hot cup of tea and a boiled egg. Packing was slow due to the collapsing inner and my taking care not to let anything blow away. I managed to get away at half past seven.

As I reached the high rock where I'd tried to pitch I looked once more for the lost tent peg, a shiny Y-peg, but without much hope. However, when I had walked on about thirty yards from the intended pitch, there was the peg by the side of the path! What a wind to blow it so far! I know it had felt like 60 mph. The peg went into the pouch pocket of my windshirt for now then I continued around the steep hill then down to the gate and on to the sign for the Bealach Walk. Now the path went uphill again to the Bealach and on my left I saw a movement - two deer loped up the hill and over the skyline.

I moved more slowly uphill of course, still in the wind and hop-ing for a sheltered spot for breakfast. As the path began to descend on the other side a sheep hollow appeared in the sandy heather bank on my right; if I sat here the bank and heather would give shelter. I sat on the sit mat, filled the kettle and put it on, with an egg handy for when it boiled. It was a relief to be out of the wind; there was a view too, beyond Killiecrankie to Blair Atholl. I decided to eat one of my wholemeal lunch rolls with the egg, for I could buy some lunch at the Old Mill Tearooms at Blair Atholl, and I made some warming lemon and ginger tea with the egg water. That felt better with something warm inside.

The path led to easy walking on a zigzag grassy track, which took me down, down, down to Killiecrankie, to a warmer temperature and a breeze in place of the wind. This descent path was not marked on my map so I wasn't sure where in Killiecrankie I was at first, and missed the Visitor Centre. The road had a wide verge here so I sat down for a drink of water and an apple with boots and socks off, also I'd removed all other warm clothing as it was surprisingly warm and sunny down here. On now to Blair Atholl, once more seeing signs for an outdoor clothing sale at the village hall, as there had been last time I was here, but I went straight to the Old Mill Tearooms, when the level crossing gates opened. A roll with corned beef and salad in, then a big slice of fruitcake and a pot of tea went down well then I was out by one o'clock. Next came the shop for a pear, some Crofters Thick Vegetable soup and a packet of chocolate Hobnobs - each biscuit gives 81 calories so six this afternoon gave me 486 much needed calories! It was good to be at Blair Atholl again with happy memories of early morning arrivals on the sleeper, and visits to the tearooms before the return journey.

By twenty past one I was heading for the lane leading to the Glen Tilt path, still in sunshine but needing the North Cape top on now. As the path reached the wooded area a lady and gent came the other way. She had a French accent - they were enjoying their holiday. I asked if she'd take a photo of me on my camera, then we went our ways and I emerged from the woodland into the wind. Further on it was hard work walking into the wind, although I was happy to be back where I had memories of walking in years gone by. It was also difficult to find somewhere out of the wind to sit down; I had two rests for snacks, the second behind a tree just past Forest Lodge. I began to wonder about my hoped-for pitch on the short, green riverside turf near the Falls of Tarf - would it be exposed and windy there? It might be better to look for a more sheltered pitch. Down by the wooden bridge below Beinn a'Ghlo looked sheltered when I stopped to inspect it; a high bank to the northeast and to the southwest a stone wall adjoining the bridge gave protection, while a streamlet ran down the bank not far away for a water supply.

Although I am three miles behind what I had planned, I have still done 17 miles today, possibly more, so I didn't do too badly, and those last miles of walking against the wind were quite tiring. Now for an early night after a lovely but windy day.

Saturday 1ˢᵗ May
- Glen Tilt to Glen Feshie:

Blue sky this morning, brilliant blue with not a cloud in sight: no longer were clouds resting on Beinn a'Ghlo. It was lovely to be pitched at the foot of one of my favourite mountains, whose various tops I enjoyed exploring a few years ago; I also feasted on the view as I had breakfast. On such a sunny morning it was worth washing the Ronhill Tracksters - they could dry over my rucksack because the other items had dried before I started walking. It was nearly three miles to the Bedford Memorial Bridge and Falls of Tarf, and never had I seen those falls look so perfect - worth another photo although I had taken one last time I was here. There was the green patch of turf on the river bank where I had camped previously and the ring ouzel had landed beside me. That had been a thrill but I had kept very still in the tent, not daring to reach for the camera. Now as the path continued on the steeply sloping bank the opposite bank was rocky, and there were two ring ouzels, although I didn't see the second one (perhaps she was on her nest) but they seemed to call and answer each other. The most common bird seen and heard today was the grouse, until I heard "chipper-chipper-chipper" and saw a snipe near the Geldie Burn. The morning, the sun, sky, river and the hills, were so wonderful that I just wandered along, taking a photo now and then, stopping for a drink of water at a stream - no need to carry it today - or to watch a peacock butterfly; the peacock seem to be the most common butterfly here.

I had a late lunch at the ruins of Bynack Lodge where I sat in the sun leaning against my rucksack by a wall while pied wagtails flitted about on the ruins. I wondered if it would be a "sandal crossing" of the river. It was, so I kept them on for the mile to the Geldie Burn, which was knee deep in one or two places. Before this I had actually met people - three ladies (Scottish) walking the other way, then there was a couple cycling along the Geldie track, and then, as I looked at another burn, considering its depth, and thought, "Sandals!" a man came and pushed his bike across. He said, "You might as well keep them on because there's a bigger one to cross in ten minutes." However, I thought, it would be longer than ten minutes for me walking, but then I realised that he meant the Geldie Burn and that was not my route; I wanted the path to the waterfall and Glen Feshie so I retraced my steps for a few minutes to the Glen Feshie path.

It took longer than expected to reach the waterfall with its1957 "Meccano" type bridge with "Cross at your own risk." sign. Probably it was due to the path being more boggy than last time that it took longer. I took a photo of the bridge with the falls below. It was not easy to see the path on the other side because the sun was in my eyes. There was another sandal crossing at the burn with the old ruined shieling above it, where we'd stopped for lunch in the sun last time (about 4 or 5 years ago); I kept my sandals on as I had decided to pitch at the next stream, which I did. It was 15 or 15 ½ miles today, not as far as I'd hoped but the last ½ hour of walking into the bright sun was not easy. This is a lovely grassy pitch with a small clear stream a few yards away and I can hear the River Feshie just below, a grouse calling and a snipe drumming. I can also hear a whistle similar to that of a golden plover but not quite the same. It keeps on: one, two, three; one, two, three. Well, it has been a really beautiful day, especially this morning. Tonight's pitch is about grid reference 43/897887.

Sunday 2nd May
- Glen Tilt and Glen Feshie to Leault near Kincraig:

The morning started cloudy with the sun trying to break through. It was nearly 8 o'clock when I woke so I must have needed the sleep. Ahead of me was that lovely walk down Glen Feshie, at first high above the river looking down steep heather banks to dark green Scots pines, white rapids and grey rock. At one burn crossing I thought I could get over dry-foot on submerged stones but a trickle of water ran down my left heel. Never mind. The remembered path was delightful, although I had forgotten the stonefalls until I saw and had two cross two of them. I wonder how the three cyclists, whom I'd met earlier, had coped with bikes across the stonefalls? Below me the river reached more level ground and divided into several strands - I remember crossing four a few years ago - so refreshing to the feet! I also remembered the old birch trees with the horse's hoof fungus on them, and the many healthy looking Scots pines. Eventually I came to the bothy and looked in - the door was open; I could hear someone moving about upstairs and a pan with two spoons in sat on a log outside. Perhaps people were working there. It was too early for a lunch stop but I had a break further on beside a stream for a drink of water and a pear. No need to carry much water today - I only needed to dip the mug into a handy burn.

The burn I'd chosen from the map for my lunch break was just after the forest, Coille an Torr. At first I'd walked on the forest track between the pines then I saw three people walking along the edge so cut across, but the edge path (not shown on the map) was also on the edge of a steep drop so care was needed. I returned to the forest where a track came down, and then a path took me northward to emerge at the burn. This was another one to ford in sandals; it was not far across and deep in places with quite a strong current. It felt much colder than others I'd crossed, probably due to snowmelt from the Cairngorms above, or the lower temperatures up there. After fording it I could really feel the warmth of the grass on the bank where I sat in the sun, feet and legs drying, while I had my lunch.

A narrow path through the heather led to an area of grass before the uninhabited Achlean, with another sandal paddle to follow. The path was diverted round Achlean to the lane, which was mostly easy walking where a carpet of pine needles had blown to the roadside. An information board told that the bank above had been the valley floor/river bank 13,000 years ago, and that the River Feshie had cut down through the sand and gravel to its present level. Later on a lady offered me a lift, which was kind of her, but I explained why I could not accept a lift, even if I wanted to, which I did not. There was an independent hostel further down the lane - I'd hoped it was a tea room, seeing bicycles outside and a "Welcome" sign, but it was not!

At Feshiebridge as I sat under a tree there was a phone signal, so I spoke to Dad, Anita and Lesley. There was also a post box so I posted the previous three maps home. I also phoned the hostel at Inverness, who have "lost" my food parcel. I hoped they'd find it by Tuesday. I continued past Loch Insh to Kincraig, where I puzzled over the map to see if there was a way to connect the A road and B road - I'd need to cross both to reach the hills. The Speybank Walk led in the wrong direction but looked, and was, very attractive, high on the wooded river bank for about a mile to a lane - not really in the wrong direction because the lane went to the B road, then a track went past the school to join the A road. Problem solved? No, it turned out that the track the other side of the road came top a full stop at a padlocked gate in a deer fence. This meant walking along the grass verge of the busy A road for at least a mile, to reach Leault farm, my original planned access to the hills. A sign on the farm gate informed people that they gave sheepdog demonstrations daily.

Sheepdogs barked, of course, as I approached the buildings, but nobody was about. I knocked at the farmhouse door to ask about camping, but there was no reply. I continued up the zigzag track quite steeply at first then at last I was level with the top of the open woodland so I crossed a small burn to wander among the trees looking for a level pitch with a view. There was a choice of two streams for water and soon the tent was pitched, water fetched and a meal was cooking. Now it has started to rain. I must wash my feet. Glen Feshie was lovely - it was good to walk the whole length of it. A most enjoyable day of 18 miles.

Monday 3ʳᵈ May 2004
- Kincraig via River Findhorn to hills before Farr:

Birdsong, spring-green grass, green leaves opening on the birch trees and the stream running by a few yards away were the first things I saw this morning. The cuckoo called a couple of times. The sun shone, on and off. I was away at 9 o'clock and, having had a good start up the steep part of the track last night, it was an easier gradient to begin this morning. Rolling, heather-clad, high moorland met blue sky ahead - what better start to the day?

There were blue-grey mountain hares than I have ever seen before; I gave up counting after six. They were mostly adults but there were two young ones. Today's birds were mainly grouse and meadow pipits, some curlew and lapwing, and a dark brown bird of prey, possibly a hen harrier, called then dropped into the heather. Later I saw a pied wagtail along the River Findhorn.

As the map showed, the track went uphill and down until it dropped to a valley where a bridge and building are shown. The little shooting hut was there but the foot suspension bridge had one end standing and the boarding lay twisted on the bank, so I put on sandals for a refreshing fording of the burn. Now a track, not marked on the map, zigzagged up a steep shoulder of the hill, making an easier ascent than walking through rough heather, then it petered out well up the shoulder before a boggy area. Another hare ran off here. I headed almost due north for the 722 metre (or 2347 feet) summit of Carn Dhu through bog and heather until the gradient eased and suddenly there was the small cairn ahead. This made an ideal viewpoint for lunch, looking towards the snow-patched Cairngorms, until a shower of rain and hail hid the sun, so I did not stop for long although the shower was soon over. A downward route NNW brought me to a streamlet that grew progressively wider so that eventually, instead of frequent crossings from side to side to walk on level grassy banks, I had to climb steeply through the heather where the banks became steeper and rocky, to reach a deer path along the edge of the deepening ravine. I've noticed before that deer seem to use these edges.

At last I could see the rounded end of the hill ahead, so I cut down to the left (I could have gone right or straight over) to reach the track. What a lovely glen with its rocky burn and scattered birch trees! I took a few photos as I went along and had a break at a small stream for a drink of water and dried banana. Too soon I was down to the River Findhorn, but this was delightful too, and there I met a flock of sheep so I took a photo with a line-up of black faces! - they had come to a halt facing me to consider whether or not to rush past, but they just stopped and posed for the photo then passed by without too much haste. Easy walking took me eastward with the breeze behind me and the blue sky reflected in the river. A peregrine called from near a rocky hill; lapwings and curlew added their voices and a pied wagtail bobbed along on the river stones. Further along two horses inspected me. Eventually a bridge took me to a narrow lane and soon a signpost showed "FARR 7 MILES." This was my turning, but I was not going as FARR this evening. After three miles, forested at first then over moorland, I left the quiet lane for a track to a peaty fast-flowing stream where there was just room for the Spacepacker with one peg going horizontally into the bank.

This has been a most enjoyable day with plenty of sun and blue sky and wild country. The weather changed in the night to wind and heavy rain, and the end of my sleeping bag got slightly damp against the lower end of the tent, not seriously though, and the wind was nowhere near as strong as on Thursday night. This has been one of the best days so far for scenery and route.

Tuesday 4th May 2004
- Farr to Inverness:

The only sound this morning was the rushing stream so close below me - even the wind had dropped; grey clouds and a little light rain were the weather this morning. The added weight of a wet tent was not very noticeable for there was very little food left now. I put almost the last of the cheese with the tomato in the last roll after breakfast and made a shopping list for Inverness, then put on waterproofs ready to go out into the dampness. During the few miles along the narrow moorland lane to Farr only one car passed me. A wheatear called from a large boulder only a few feet away and looked at me fearlessly, while a nearby grouse "go-backed" in panic. I tried to imagine the dark heathery hills and grey sky as they'd be with purple or green heather and blue sky. Lower down some gorse added colour to the scene. I came level with the odd shaped forest shown on both maps, so was now able to put the Inverness map to the front of the map-case, then it was another forested mile to the end of the lane. Near Farr I was surprised to see two llamas appear in a wood to my right, each with a small leather head-collar on. I took a photo of them. There was a large patch of wood anemones in the wood too, not, obviously, eaten by these animals.

My next surprise was a notice on a telegraph pole "SHOP 1 mile," with some of the items listed that they sold. This meant no turning left on the narrow lane at Farr but staying on the B road to Inverarnie in order to visit the shop, but this road had hardly any traffic. A yellow-hammer and a thrush sang and there were calls of curlew, lapwings and oystercatchers. I was beginning to think it was a very long mile to the shop, when I saw it, just round the corner on the B861 Inverness road, almost hidden by a wood across the road. It had all I needed to satisfy my hunger after long days of wild walking with few people and no shops. I bought a ginger cake (Walkers Old-fashioned Gingerbread Cake), shortbread fingers, a ripe banana ("you can have that" the lady said) a Mars bar, a roll and three eggs. Yes, the helpful lady was happy to sell me three eggs so I popped out to the rucksack for an egg box. She was very friendly and asked about the walk. I am so relieved that the shop was there because I saw no shops in Inverness, near the hostel, that sold these things. I went on along the road, having posted a film and binned the rubbish bag, until a green track into the forest looked inviting so I went just inside the forest for lunch, hanging the damp flysheet over the barrier to dry.

I arrived in Inverness after about 14½ miles at half past four, before the shops closed. I found the hostel after enquiring at the TIC, checked that the food parcel had not been found, drew £30 from Nationwide (near the hostel), bought a Lairg map and ½ litre meths from Graham Tiso's, two carrots, milk and Ayrshire cheese from M&S, opposite Eastgate Backpackers Hostel, and Mornflake Oat Bran, fruit bar, nut roast and yoghurt from the health food shop next door (Holland & Barrett), and an Aberdeen Angus beefburger from the market hall for tomorrow night. In my search for suitable shops I'd seen a fish and chip shop a few minutes' walk away so after unpacking, stowing food away in the fridge and having a mug of tea, I went and bought haddock and chips for £3.50, which I brought back and ate at the hostel, followed by the yoghurt and more tea. The friendly hostel offers free tea and coffee. Next I got the LEJOG form signed at reception, had a shower, washed some clothes and wrote a postcard.

It had been good to see Inverness and Kessock Bridge from the gorse-lined road above - another landmark and another stage almost completed! The gorse had its fragrant coconut smell intensified by the vast quantity and there was also the occasional violet. In today's diary I jumped from Inverarnie to Inverness…while I was stopped for lunch on the green forest ride a black dog was suspicious and barked while its owner called and whistled to it. I ignored the dog, and the dog ignored its owner, and I tucked into my roll, ginger cake and shortbread. The dog eventually gave up and returned to its owner. The flysheet, being in the shade, dripped but didn't dry very much. This road walking with some ease on grass verges was not too bad but the last mile into Inverness was a long one, as streets usually are, but no sore feet or anything. On the way into Inverness I'd asked a man which was the quickest way to the city centre; he told me then said there had been snow on "the Ben" this morning. That must have been Ben Wyvis. Now here I am, ready for bed, and for tomorrow's walk to Evanton.

Tuesday 5th May 2004
- Inverness to Evanton, Black Rock, via Munlochy:
I got up at 7 o'clock and went for breakfast at 7.30, only to find that the kitchen doesn't open until 8 o'clock, so I decided to wash my hair, then my towel, to pass the half hour. Breakfast was the Mornflake Oat Bran cereal, scrambled egg cooked in the microwave and two mugs of tea (one teabag). I packed the clothes that had dried overnight, and everything else, then after talking I got away about twenty past nine. The first call was "The Baker's Oven" for three

brown rolls, then Graham Tiso's, who were supposed to open at 9.30 but were not open at 9.35; I was only going to enquire if they kept individual sachets of Nikwax or other boot dressing as I've finished mine. Finally I went to the station to see if my sleeper ticket had arrived - it had - and to enquire about trains from Wick or Thurso for my return, so having left the station at 9.50 I was running a bit late.

Now for the walk round the shore road to the bridge, which the lady at the TIC said was accessible there - no, it was NOT - I had to walk under the bridge then round to the next roundabout but got there in the end. (I later found out at the Backpackers AGM that John & Bettie Bryce had seen me approaching the bridge but were unable to stop and speak!) It was a showery crossing then a cycleway dropped to North Kessock, where a useful shop provided an apple, a tomato and a Mars bar, all for 50p, then I continued, the showers now over it seemed. I suddenly realised that I was following a cycleway for Tore; although in the right direction there was no reasonable route beyond Tore, so I went via Bogallan to Munlochy, a pleasant village where I stopped for lunch on some grass by a tub of tulips and a Black Isle Footpaths information board. I remember that Sally Thomas (book) on her walk didn't think much of Munlochy, perhaps due to the weather. Anyway, I'd put the tent over the lower wires of the fence to dry (upper one barbed) with the farmer mowing silage in the field behind and I sat comfortably eating my roll, cheese, tomato and gingerbread then I heard a whistle and a call and looked up to see a man at the house across the road. He asked if I'd like a cup of tea to which I replied, "That would be nice, thank you very much," and had just put my socks and boots back on when he came across with a mug of not tea but coffee, which was nice and hot, and said, "You can leave the mug on the sill." However, when I was ready a lady, his wife no doubt, had just got out of a car, crossed the road and gone in, so I knocked and thanked her when I returned the mug. What nice people I meet!

From Munlochy narrow lanes led gently upward between beech trees and green fields, then a trig pillar appeared in a field to my left as it started to rain again. This was not the top of the hill; the map showed 122 metres at the trig. I continued in sunshine and showers in a north westerly direction until I saw the name GLASFIELD at the end of a wooded track. Too far! Crasky had not shown a name and the lane junction where I should have turned was not signposted either so I'd walked an extra third of a mile and had to return to the lane. Along this lane I had a break with boots off at four o'clock for a finger of shortbread and drink of water. Chiff-chaffs called, then I heard thunder so set off again, coming to Calbokie, the last village before Cromarty Bridge and the last on the map so now on to Landranger sheet 21.

Before the bridge a road sign read "John O'Groats 109" - another landmark so I took a photo, although it will be more than 109 miles for me. It seemed a long crossing (about 1½ miles) with a plaque half way across saying that the Cromarty Bridge was opened on 12th April 1979. Every time I looked at the view it was Cromarty Firth and grey cloud; there had been a thunderstorm before I crossed but it didn't last long. Now my hoped-for path on the map DID exist, not used a lot obviously, but it ran between trees to a kissing gate on the railway, then over a wire fence, a green track with blue, white and pink wild hyacinths. Past a farm a track led to a lane and 2½ miles to Black Rock Camping Park, with a shop at Evanton too, for milk etc. I was not charged for camping. I settled down to a good meal of Aberdeen Angus burger, carrot, nettles and mash and on approach to the shower block a rabbit scuttled away. 17 ½ miles today - a satisfying day, once over Kessock Bridge.

Thursday 6th May 2004
- Evanton to "sheep bothy" beyond Clach Goil:
There was heavy rain in the night and early morning but it cleared to give blue sky before I got up. Black Rock is a pleasant campsite, all very clean with good, hot water and, above all, it is quiet. The owner let me camp free as the walk is for charity (otherwise £5). A "resident rabbit" feeds near the toilet/shower block so I saw it every time I went over or came out. When I left the site I popped back to the shop for some mash to go with the nut "roast" tonight then went along the B road, a short section of which is a path parallel with the railway. Alness would be the station nearest to Evanton. Now the road was lined with tall beech trees with the sun shining through their new spring leaves. Cow parsley is beginning to flower here and there, and a few bluebells, violets and stitchwort. Although it was not busy, I was relieved to turn off the road, after a lovely stretch where an old bridge crosses the River Alness, at an old lodge-type house where a lady in the garden said "Hello."

This lane ran mostly between trees before Ardross, with its castle gates with eagles on (I think they were eagles) but the castle was out of sight. I had my lunch inside the grassy churchyard as there was nowhere else to sit except the lawns outside the castle gates! The sun ½ shone and it was quite warm. Later the valley widened with scattered farms and cottages then the lane ended eventually near the "chambered cairn, remains of" on the map. I took a photo through the wire fence but not much to see except a stone or two.

I went up to Woodside Cottage where the track/path on the map leaves for wood and hill but couldn't see any sign of it so I knocked at the door. "It goes up there through the wood and crosses the burn. Sometimes you can see it and sometimes you can't," the man told me. Well, if I couldn't see the part going through the wood I'd have difficulties so I decided to go round the forest to reach it. I went down to the forest track with a Walkers Welcome sign here. This was an open, sunny track between larches and Scots pines, gently rising. Where the forest ends I should be able to ascend beside the burn and head northeast for the Clach Goil track - and there was an unlocked gate in the deer fence so I followed the fence up beside the forest BUT as I got higher I could see a deer fence crossing my line of travel then, fortunately, a gate. First I had to get down a steep bank to the fast-flowing burn, find a place to ford safely between the boulders in sandals, then up the other bank and along the fence to the gate. (I was back in boots now). A pathless boggy area lay between me and the expected path so I picked my way in the right general direction (NE), keeping an eye on where the path should be coming from until a faint raised line, as of a low bank, appeared ahead - was that it? It was!

A wet indentation would be a better description than a path, which led to the large stone or rock of Clach Goil and continued boggily down northward. It took some concentration on foot placing, but was still better than trying to walk alongside. It had a real atmosphere of bygone days with Clach Goil as an ancient landmark seen from afar by drovers or others walking this way. A building with rusty-red roof could be seen some way ahead ...and still Clach Goil was visible when I looked back. I had planned to pitch somewhere about here; 16 miles or 18 miles I'd written on my itinerary, but due to the ubiquitous wetness the obvious place was by the building which was in an oasis of sheep-nibbled grass. This was after 16 ½ miles. At last I reached it, Clach Goil still on the skyline. A look inside the empty cottage showed a sheepy floor, two main rooms, a smaller one centre back, formed by a wooden partition from the other rooms, and a ruined outbuilding. There is no glass in the windows.

I've seen one golden plover on the hill - a snipe nearby has just reminded me. After pitching the tent on the short green turf I fetched peaty water and fresh nettles then had tea as the sun shone into the tent. It was nut roast, simmered in a pan, with nettles and mash then butterscotch delight. Now it is ten o'clock and still light. Here ends another good day.

Friday 7ᵗʰ May 2004
- Between Clach Goil and Ardgay to Lairg, Dunroamin Campsite:

At six o'clock on a grey-skied morning the first sound was of sheep munching nearby. I dozed off until 7.20, when the sun was breaking through the clouds and the sheep had gone. There was absolute silence and peace - not even the burn could be heard. I set off at 9.25 in sandals because the first thing I had to do was to ford the burn, which turned out to be only ankle deep here, then with boots on again I continued along a wet and boggy path as yesterday. Some sections of the path were surprisingly clear and almost dry. The sky was now blue and meadow pipits darted about. Eventually, after a section of unclear path ("Sometimes you can see it and sometimes you can't!") I'd continued in the same general direction, then thought it must be time to cut down towards the burn where there should be a track on the bank by now. I made my way down and there it was. The track was easy walking, of course, with sheep and lambs running ahead of me. The little house on the far bank by the forest was accessible only by a foot suspension bridge and looked as if it was only used for storage; things seemed to be piled in front of a window. Further on the river dropped down a waterfall into a gorge with birch trees and gorse, but you couldn't get near for a photo of the falls, although you could hear the water all right. This was a delightful part of the walk. Now the track went on past some trees and a house and down to the road where the Kyle of Sutherland, I think it was, reflected the blue sky. "Welcome to Sutherland" said a sign in the shade of the trees. Another landmark.

At 1.15pm I reached Ardgay, found the shop and bought some more of that delicious Walkers Gingerbread Cake, also an apple, a tomato, chocolate and a postcard, then I stopped for lunch a bit further on near the railway bridge on some grass. When I got up to go

I realised that I'd left my poles outside the shop so I'm glad it was only a few minutes away - they were now inside. After another mile I reached Bonar Bridge, where I posted three maps home, bought, wrote and posted a card to Impressions, and bought a calorific apple and cream puff turnover - delicious - to keep me going for the miles to Lairg.

There were yellowhammers, yellow gorse, yellow dandelions, yellow marsh marigolds and cream primroses, also a few violets. This morning I'd seen a golden plover in the heather, then there were lapwings and a curlew, and near Lairg there were buzzards.

I took a photo of the bridge at Bonar Bridge then looked at the time, realising that I should not have time to go over the hill then down for the four mile road walk into Lairg in reasonable time so I should have to go all the way by road; this morning's wet miles of bog and heather had taken some time. However, I could turn off at Invershin on to the B road, a narrow lane, which goes via the Falls of Shin to Lairg. It was a really warm, sunny afternoon - T-shirt and sun cream - but I could have done with more water so rationed it out.

It was good to arrive at Lairg and reach the campsite by about 7pm. Again there were kind people here who said that if I was doing the walk for charity there would be nothing to pay. First I filled the water bottle and had a drink, then pitched the tent and opened the food parcel, went for a wash and washed the Craghoppers trousers that I'd been wearing. I had a good meal, washed up and phoned Dad and Anne & Chris, then Trevor, and had to change the phone battery during the call to Anne. Chris suggested a slightly different route to Kinbrace, which looks all right, missing Loch Choire but joining the track further on.

Will my trousers dry? - it is raining now at ten o'clock. The rain is only very light and the forecast for tomorrow is better. Now I'd better put the maps away and settle down to sleep after a good day of 18 miles.

Saturday 8th May 2004
- Lairg to An Crom Allt:

Heavy rain drummed on the flysheet during the night and the day dawned grey but mild and dry. Muesli and boiled egg for breakfast; again, last year's toast from the parcel tasted quite fresh. It has all kept well, some toast being crisp and some more chewy but all fresh and "toast-tasting." Before packing I left my trousers spread over the tent to dry while I went down to the shops unladen. From Mace I needed rolls, cheese, eggs, tomato, apple and banana and from the newsagents I needed the other two maps to replace those in the missing food parcel - I had not been sure which food parcel they were in until opening the parcel at Lairg last night and finding only the John O'Groats map.

I had heard the cuckoo again both last night and while having breakfast.

After a strenuous but enjoyable day yesterday, today was going to be a relaxed one. Although I'd put grid ref. 632185 down for a possible pitch for tonight it did not matter whether I stopped before or after that, as long as I am at Thurso on Wednesday to meet Anne and Chris. The route Chris had mentioned on the phone last night forked right off my route and passed Ben Armine; this looks interesting and I have already walked part of the Loch Choire route back from Ben Klibreck two years ago so I'll try it. Along the A836 (single track) road larks were singing and there were yellowhammers and curlew and another cuckoo could be heard. Along the open forest track there were mostly meadow pipits and a snipe. I walked at a steady, easy pace, stopping when I felt like it, turning the drying trousers on the rucksack and taking a photo of primroses, violets or marsh marigolds, the latter beside a stream, or in it, taken from a bridge on the Dalnessie Forest track. At lunchtime I sat comfortably on a mound of rock and tussocks then changed into the dry trousers before moving on, as I prefer walking in trousers with pockets.

After four miles of track I reached Dalnessie; by now the sun was shining between the clouds and some pale blue sky appeared, but this sunshine did not last very long. Never mind - there was no rain or wind. Dalnessie was an isolated group of buildings including three houses with no sign of life except some washing on a line and the clucking of some free range hens. There were also several golden plover quite near and I actually saw one flying - usually they appear from behind a rock or their heads appear over a clump of heather or rushes. The burn, further on, was populated by plenty of dippers.

The grassy track was pleasanter to walk on than the stony one before Dalnessie, then a deer fence came into view. Not a padlocked gate, I hoped. It was not padlocked but the gate was new and stiff to open - I had to raise the high metal gate with my left foot and hand in order to slide back the catch, having first got it past the metal flap that has to be lifted. About ten minutes or so later there was another deer fence with gate, but the same method did not work - the slider/bolt just would not budge at all. It would be possible to climb the lower sheep fence (square wire mesh) but not the higher deer fence with a heavy rucksack on, though perhaps I could empty the rucksack and push things one at a time under the gate, followed by the flat rucksack - but further gate opening efforts first. There was no "handle" to grip to slide the bolt back so what could I use to lever it back? A bleached white deer bone, part of a rib, lay on the ground so I tried it: a very slight movement brought the "slider" past the "faller" but a bit of bone broke off. Another try, at the same time doing the boot lift - again, a slight movement and a bit more bone broke off. Try again - nothing. Lift with foot, with left hand too, lever with bone - another slight movement but not enough. Must keep on trying - plenty of bone left for only tiny bits have broken off. Lift again and push back really hard with the bone - the gate was free at last! This must have taken 10-15 minutes. What a relief! I shut the gate with difficulty, only just managing to get the bolt in far enough to hold it, and laid the bone carefully by the gatepost, very thankful for that vital tool, then picked up the pack and poles and walked on into the wild country.

At the confluence of two burns the building marked on the map was a shed with a window and a corrugated iron roof, high on a grassy bank. I followed the east burn until it turned east about ¾ mile beyond 632185 and, as I stopped on a suitable level grassy area I saw two deer ahead, then two more. We looked at each other then they loped off up the hillside. They had been only about 40 yards away. The tent was soon pitched on the bank of An Crom Allt, and I collected water standing on a rock below the bank, dipping my mug into the peat coloured burn. I enjoyed a leisurely meal of chicken, leek, peas, red peppers and rice in a sauce of chicken soup, then apricot and apple crumble and custard. During the meal the wind changed so I changed zips. After the meal I listened to Scottish Country dance music then the music of the burn beside me. A leisurely day of 11 miles with a heavy pack

Sunday 9th May
- An Crom allt to below Cnoc an Chrom Uillt:

The forecast gave cloud and mist for the north coast of Scotland but there was cloud and mist here too; I unzipped the tent to find that the nearest hills were out of sight. However, soon after breakfast the sun was shining into the tent and very few clouds remained. If it hadn't been for the four deer yesterday I think I might have forded the burn further on before pitching - it would have saved a few minutes' walk before changing into sandals to do it this morning. Anyway, I was soon across with feet dried and booted and continued slowly and squelchily upward. The morning grew warmer so I stopped for a drink at the burn on the way up to where the path sweeps round a large area of bog and heather then it descends through heather to ford a wider burn opposite Green Face - an unusual name in this part of Scotland, but the face of the hill is green. There used to be a suspension bridge here; three upright poles are still standing. As usual, crossing in sandals was very refreshing to the feet and refreshment to the mind was provided by the marvellous variety sounds produced by the water running over or round the many different sized stones; it was like listening to music.

"Thou flowing water pure and clear,
Make music for thy Lord to hear. Alleluia!"
St Francis of Assisi.

I sat in the sun to let my feet dry while I ate a finger of shortbread, then the path climbed steadily but not steeply as it followed above the burn. The heat increased - not too hot but rather warm for going uphill on an uneven path. A frog and then a lizard jumped and scuttled into the heather; later in the day another two frogs and one more lizard, which had been basking in the sun on the track below Ben Armine, hurried away from my footfalls.

Although I'd intended to reach the building at the next confluence for lunch I decided to stop here on the track, where there was a slight breeze, because in warm still air lots of small brown flying beetles came and landed on hair, clothing, mapcase or anything else. No bites or stings but there were just so many of them. I thought I'd manage to ford the next burn in boots on the stones but when I was almost across I stepped on a submerged stone and my right boot got a trickle of water down the heel. Now the track was less boggy and climbed slowly to the south side of Ben Armine. A different view would be ahead soon.

Yes, over the low lying ground ahead and below me were low misty hills and higher ones more distant and blue. As I turned the corner below the rocky face of Ben Armine there was a scattering of blue lochs to be seen. I used the last exposure of the film for Ben Armine then removed the film to replace it with the final one - a bit sad really, that this is the final film of the walk. There were other boot prints on the path now, as well as those of deer, but I saw nobody all day. The track undulated with occasional clear streams to drink from, then at last it descended to the track that comes past Ben Klibreck from Crask (enjoyed 2 years ago).

On I went with the sun behind me until I reached the burn where I planned to camp, An Crom Allt below Cnoc a Chrom Uillt. A high green bank on a bend looked ideal and the sun shone in as I cooked macaroni cheese with leek and broccoli then at 9.15pm I took a photo of the sunset from inside the tent. The colours are still in the sky now at 10.15 as a snipe chippers nearby. What a lovely day, especially the quietness of that vast area of wilderness where hardly a bird called - all resting in the heat! - and the music of the water. I am now ready for sleep and it is still not dark. 14½ miles today.

Monday 10th May
- Below Cnoc an Chrom Uillt to Forsinard:

The lovely sunset and red sky last night were not a shepherd's delight this time it seems; the cloud is low on he hills and the warm sun of yesterday is not to be seen, but there are still good views below cloud level. The pegs came out clean from their firm bed of sand beneath the grass. It was surprisingly chilly when I set off so I actually put on thin gloves and the North Cape top is on under the windshirt too. I soon warmed up walking briskly along the track; deer had also walked that way. At Gearnsary, round the hill, the building on the map was a corrugated iron roofed cottage used for storage, I think - the windows were blocked with stones - and there were many other ruins and remains of buildings so it must have been a fair sized group at one time. I took a photo; the red roof and green trees gave some colour on a grey day. Before the track reached the road I stopped at a stream for a drink of water and to add another mugful to the bottle.

Where the first bridge crosses an inlet of Loch Badanloch there was a sandy beach fenced with old twisted pine from peat bogs and four rowing boats drawn up, black edged with green, and a notice about their use, warning also of sudden squalls on the loch. Also I had read another sign earlier about "20 mph for the sake of our road and your vehicle" - our road being the Loch Choire track. Now I was on the B road toward Kinbrace, or rather on the grass and gravel verges where deer had also preferred the softer going. This was quick and easy walking to Harvieston where I had lunch on the river bank, just below an obviously new metal bridge. I wonder what happened to the old one. I had managed 9 miles before lunch so should have an earlyish finish today.

It seemed strange to see and hear a train moving along the hillside near Kinbrace. Soon I was over the level crossing at Kinbrace station. Kinbrace consists of the station, a few houses, one of which looked as if it used to be a shop, and what might have been a smithy with a chimney and two pairs of double doors and one single door, also, up on the A road, a primary school. The A897 to Melvich is a narrow with passing places and is very quiet. There are forests, low hills of 1000-1200feet, lochs, moorland and the railway. I saw two deer under pine trees by the railway. Sometimes I could walk on grass and gravel at the roadside but sometimes it sloped away too steeply or was too stony. I passed Dubh Loch at 4 o'clock - too early to pitch - and went on to Forsinard, which has RSPB Visitor Centre, a hotel, a few houses and the station with level crossing. About ¾ mile beyond here a man on a bicycle spoke and asked if I was going to John O'Groats. I said I was and asked him if he knew of anywhere nearby where I could camp. He pointed out somewhere by a bridge 4 miles ahead on the map but after 17 miles already I preferred to stop sooner, so he suggested going back to the RSPB Visitor Centre and kindly phoned someone there (he was a warden) to say that I'd be coming. He said I could camp in the garden of South Station Cottage (RSPB office) and get water from next door, which was very kind of him. Back I went for the ¾ mile and pitched beside the shed in unmown grass, soft and comfortable, and there were also a few nettles to go in my pea and bacon soup. In the evening I phoned Anne, Maurice, Dad, Joan Cockram and Tony Wilson - I hope that's not too many! but I'd had two nights without a signal. I am looking forward to seeing Anne and Chris at Thurso on Wednesday.

Today I walked 16½ miles plus the 1½ extra = 18 miles.

Tuesday 11th May 2004
- Forsinard to Melvich, Halladale Inn camp site:

After a comfortable night I woke to rain falling softly on the flysheet. A train arrived at twenty to eight. I hoped to be able to pack a dry tent but, after a dry spell, it rained again. There was one thing to be decided: should I get off quickly to Melvich to be there before the shop closed, or should I go to the RSPB Visitor Centre and risk no shop? RSPB Visitor Centre - I shouldn't like to miss it since I am so near and I could still possibly make it to the shop before it closes.

An interesting video of the local area and birds lasted 40 minutes. It showed hen harrier, curlew, snipe, greenshank, red and black throated divers, dippers, meadow pipits, larks, and the golden eagle as an autumn visitor, also the mountain hare. It was well worth staying for. I had a look at the display of photos and had a chat with the young lady warden and two visitors from Chester, who all sponsored me. It was gone 11am when I left, after a photo on the station platform outside the Centre, so I put on the pace for the first 4 miles. At about 5 miles there is a rocky gorge on the left, where I stopped for a drink of water and flapjack, then left the rucksack while I went over to the edge to take a photo with lots of primroses on the far bank. Although on an A road there were very few vehicles; it was narrow with a grass verge that was mostly walkable. I had decided to turn off this road where a lane leaves to cross the Halladale River and runs along the other side.

Lunch was down by the bridge, sheltered from the breeze, then I continued up the lane past various houses, farms and cottages, gorse and bushes. A black and white collie approached for a friendly word, an elderly farmer walking behind. "He'll go up to anyone," he said. At the farm at the far end of the lane two farmers were looking at a pen of sheep and lambs. I asked about the path shown on the map for Melvich. "Yes, it goes through the open gate there. Just follow the track all the way to Melvich." Soon after the open gate the path passed through a muddy pool. How deep? Go round through the boggy area, treading on clumps of rushes. For once "Where rushes grow man may go" let me down, and down went my boots to give soggy socks. Right, back to test the pool depth with poles and to tiptoe gradually forward where it we not too deep - ah, managed it!

Where the track forded two burns I should not have minded if my left boot went under again, but of course both were shallow or passable on stones. The sun shone again; the gorse was bright, the sky a pale blue and a rabbit lolloped across the track. With banks of heather the track ascended between two low rocky hills then the sea was in sight, with the Halladale River running towards it through green fields of sheep and lambs. The track went up past the cemetery, through a farmyard, Kirkton, with friendly collies, and then soon out to the road and to Melvich. The pub with campsite was not far but first I looked for the shop where the P was on the map, and a little further on, but there was no sign of it, not even a post-box, so I returned to the Halladale Inn to see about camping, then pitched, washed some clothes, had soup, couscous and vegetables then had a shower and hairwash before going to the pub for a nice filling pudding - strawberry jam sponge pudding and custard. I'm still sitting at the table writing this. I did enjoy that pud!

I have looked at the map for tomorrow and decided that the extra food is urgently needed so I'll go to the shop, which I'm told is a mile to the west, then continue with tomorrow's walk to Thurso to meet Anne and Chris. I can return from the shop via the river bridge and track to cut out a loop of road and rejoin the Thurso road, but I must make a fairly early start. Today's 15½ miles passed quickly - I was here by 5.30pm and had plenty of time to do things. I'll go back to the tent now.

Wednesday 12th May 2004
- Melvich to Thurso:
At 6 o'clock the sun shone into the tent, then a cloud passed in front of it, then sunshine again. I was able to sit in the sun for breakfast then I put my T-shirt over the fence to dry and the smaller items on the guylines while I went for a wash, also washed the Tracksters since they would soon dry. The shop, although a mile the wrong way, was a necessity so at 9 o'clock I dropped the toilet/shower key through the letterbox as requested, then walked up the road with the T-shirt over the rucksack to finish drying. I looked down the road to the right - Portskerra - and saw a Post Office sign, so that would be the shop. What had they that would refuel me after these four days without a shop? Walkers Sultana Cake (no gingerbread here) an apple, 2 bananas, a morning roll, a Mars bar, and a bar of chocolate for tomorrow. Outside I posted the last film, ate one of

the bananas, binned the banana skin (to find some wrapped out-of-date morning rolls - 2? - which would be extra fuel), so I packed the food and strode off - it was now 9.40am.

I took the track to Melvich beach. The north coast of Scotland is another landmark. Where the path passed through a kissing gate there were lots of small, short-stemmed cowslips, not enough for a photo but a good scattering of them there. A grassy path led to sand dunes and a footbridge over the Halladale River, then past one or two smaller houses and a big house on the far side. A heron flew over the river. The footpath was supposed to leave the track on a sharp bend; there was nothing to be seen in the heather. Perhaps, if I set off in the right direction, it would appear higher up. No - after a while I was still making my way over heather and bog with cross-leaved heath and some bog myrtle (I love its smell and squeezed a leaf between my finger and thumb). There was the little lochan over there so it would be best to head past that to the road for quicker movement or I'd be late at Thurso, over 14 miles away, for meeting Anne and Chris. I soon reached the road.

There were views of blue sea and sky with green fields of sheep and lambs or heather and gorse. Somewhere along here was another landmark - the "Welcome to Caithness" sign. The road passed throughReay, with the shop that Bryan Crick had mentioned so I bought some plain chocolate biscuits, 89p, and a tomato. After Reay was Dounreay then just beyond Dounreay I sat down at the end of a track beside some cottages for lunch - not much choice of where to sit down round here - I had cheese and tomato roll and 4 chocolate biscuits; each one is 87 calories so that will help. I seemed to be making good time.

There were still lapwings and curlews, also larks and meadow pipits and before Reay a stonechat with black head and chestnut breast chirping away from a gorse bush. I could smell the gorse too. After Bridge of Forss there was a large rookery with much cawing in the trees.

After 4 o'clock the traffic, presumably from Dounreay, increased so no longer was it peaceful walking, but Thurso was in sight. Unfortunately the verge was too lumpy to be walkable so hard road it had to be for some distance. I came past the campsite into Thurso, round to the TIC and there were Anne and Chris - I heard Anne's voice. It was lovely to see them. We went to the Co-op for food requirements for our evening meal then back to the campsite. That made a total of 19 miles today.

There are lovely views of the sea but the sky has clouded over now. A good meal, good company, a shower and another snack (delicious Yeo Valley yoghurt) and now I am ready for bed. It should be a good walk tomorrow.

Thursday 13th May
- Thurso to Dunnet Head:

The grey sky gave drizzle then slightly wetter rain during breakfast, so we packed wet tents. I should have taken a photo of the tents last night when the sun was shining. Before setting off round the coast I needed to buy a couple of rolls from a baker's then post three maps back from the Post office (71p). That done, we found a sign "Coast Path" although the path itself soon vanished in nettles and other greenery but at first it was easy walking with banks of primroses sloping down to the cliffs and marsh marigolds here and there. Later we edged along beside a fence of wire with vertical flagstones before deciding that the beach would give easier walking. On the beach, flat slabs of rock (from which the flagstones came) lay in shattered steps, with seaweed lower down the beach and shells in spaces between the rocks. This was Murkle Bay, quite a small bay, then we climbed up to a green track and went on to Castle Hill and Castletown, where we at first thought that the remains of a windmill were an old broch. Round the corner by the harbour were a couple of picnic tables where we had our lunch. As we finished, a blind man came along with his shining black guide dog, Gable, and rescue dog, Morven. The man's name was Jessan; he was born in 1936 further west along the coast. (Chris said he he'd seen the house on a previous visit to Scotland). Jessan asked about the walk and even gave me a Scottish £1 note towards the walk charities. He said he usually walked 10 or 11 miles a day with his dogs and showed us a poem someone had written about him doing a sponsored walk of 16 miles with guide dog, Quill. He said he had enjoyed talking to us, and we had to him.

A few minutes later we came to a stone with the words "Beach path opened in the year 2000 by Jessan." What a coincidence! We followed the path behind the dunes then over the dunes to the beach, a lovely beach of firm sand - wonderful walking. Next we went up to the wildlife visitor centre near the caravan site and saw what birds and animals were to be found in the area. They did not serve pots of tea, which we had hoped for, but told us to try the hotel at Dunnet, which we did, and enjoyed that pot of tea, sitting comfortably, with a plate of biscuits too, giving us renewed energy to continue to Dunnet Head. Anne, however, felt tired so I suggested that we walk up the road to the lighthouse, pitch and have a meal, then have an evening walk along the headland cliffs. All agreed.

On the way, at Brough, we saw a lady returning to her house with a basket of brown eggs so I asked if she would sell me a couple as I only had one left. "I'll give you two," she said and gave me two lovely deep brown ones. We do meet nice people. She also asked us if we'd like a cup of tea so we explained that we'd only just had a pot at the hotel. We went on past St John's Loch with masses of co-conut gorse, up the moorland road with the lochs, sky and sea views until Chris suggested getting water at a loch to save coming back for it. We filled water bottles then continued to a tall stone near the lighthouse, "Dunnet Head, the most northerly point of mainland Britain" were the words on it. We asked some other visitors to take a photo of the three of us there on both Anne's and my camera. Next we found a pitch on soft springy grass to the east of the light-house, had our meal then went for our evening walk. First we went as far to the north as one could safely go next to the lighthouse, then we walked a little way down the west coast, stopping to watch sea birds on the cliffs and one puffin, which delighted us, going in and out of a hole.

The sky was hazy now and the sea silver and calm, the Orkneys grey shapes a few miles off the coast. Also from the viewpoint we had seen Cape Wrath in the far distance. What a lovely day we have had! Now a snipe is drumming and lighthouses are flashing.

All is peaceful. Goodnight.

Friday 14th May 2004
- Dunnet Head to John O'Groats:

That really was a beautiful night's pitch on Dunnet Head. We left just after nine o'clock and followed a path round above the loch then walked down past the gorse and the house where the lady gave me the eggs, then turned left at Brough, where we stopped to remove warm clothing now that we were lower down. It was still cloudy but dry with none of the rain that had been forecast for northern Scotland. The lane passed fields of sheep, cows and calves, then passed a loch with a swan nesting on an island, with an old watermill (no wheel to be seen) nearby. Further on we turned left at the primary school then a track took us back to the breezy coast. We found a grassy bank to shelter us for our lunch break; standing, we could feel the breeze, but sitting, we were sheltered. Anne took a photo of me with one of our last views of Dunnet Head behind me. We also took a photo of the Castle of Mey as we passed. Too soon the track took us back to the road, the A836, which had very little traffic, we were pleased to find, but before this we had stopped for a mid-morning break on some grass between scattered houses on the coastal lane, then came to a bungalow where two West Highland white terriers barked at our approach and a lady came to talk to us. She said she would give me something for the walk and went to the house so I asked if she'd fill a water bottle too, as we only had a little boiled loch water left. She kindly filled all our bottles so we had a supply for the day - we did not expect to find any tearooms today. Today's flowers have been heath milkwort (on Dunnet Head) then red campion, primroses, and celandines.

The names we'd read on the map met us on road signs as we walked eastward towards John O'Groats and at last we could see John O'Groats ahead with its white hotel building, familiar from photographs. That last bit of road walking was hard on the feet as the narrow grass verge was too uneven to walk on. We talked to a grey and a chestnut horse over a fence, then we stopped for a final break and a drink of water before the last stretch to the T junction, where we turned left, northward, for John O'Groats. We made for the hotel first to register my arrival as a LEJOG walker, having crossed the finishing line outside at 4.30pm. Also Chris and Anne took photos of me at the John O'Groats milepost. We had a cup of coffee at the hotel before going to the campsite, which is right beside the sea. Anne and I left our rucksacks at the site office before going up the road to the shop before it closed. I wanted milk, an apple, gingerbread and stamps; I also got a tin of peas to share with Anne & Chris - I think they shared broccoli with me. I sent a couple of postcards. I should be excited but I really felt that I'd "Done it at Dunnet!" and would do it again at Duncansby Head, the most north-easterly point, but it was satisfying to have reached John O'Groats.

Back at the campsite with the tents sheltered on the west side by a grassy bank, which also had rhubarb growing on it, we cooked our meals then went to wash up, wash selves and I washed my socks and the peaty legs of my trousers before we went back to the John O'Groats Hotel for a celebratory drink - no celebratory meal here because they only do pizzas, so we'll have a meal on Orkney tomorrow. When we returned it was still not dark but it was too late to write my diary, so I'm writing it at six o'clock on Saturday morning. I've had two congratulatory text messages from Bryan Crick and Geoff Gadsby, so I phoned them to thank them, also phoned Anita and Dad to say that I'd arrived!

It is very satisfying to have completed the walk, although it will really be completed at Duncansby Head. I have enjoyed the walk tremendously, but I am sorry it is over. However, we shall have a couple of interesting days on Orkney. Now I can hear the waves breaking just below and a wren is singing loudly from a bush on the bank.

I'd better get up and get packed before 8.45 when we have to be ready for the ferry.

Saturday 15th May
- On the ferry for the Day Trip to Orkney:

At 5.30 in the morning we were woken by the sound of a boat starting - perhaps not surprising as that corner of the campsite beside the sea is very near the jetty. After lying there for a few minutes I decided that I was sufficiently awake to sit up and write yesterday's diary. After that I had my breakfast. The ferry office is next to the campsite so we aimed to be there soon after 8.30 for the 9am ferry.

While actually in the queue we decided to buy the Maxi Tour ticket, £35, which takes you on a coach from the ferry on South Ronaldsay, over the Churchill Barriers, four of them, concrete blocks making a causeway with the road connecting the islands. We had a half hour stop at Kirkwall so went to the information centre for details of campsites and places for meals. I also bought a cream bun and a tomato at a shop nearby - time later in the day to see St Magnus Cathedral. Next was something I had looked forward to seeing, after reading about it some time ago - Skarra Brae, the 5000 year old Neolithic village. Although I had read about it and seen photos of the stone box beds, dressers and central fireplaces, it was really fascinating to see the group of dwellings and the replica house that had been built for people to be able to walk through. I bought the booklet (£2.50) and admission was £3.30 for me. These bus tours had a reduced entry fee and senior citizens also paid less, which included a visit to Skaill House next to Skarra Brae, which was also interesting. We went on to the Ring of Brodgar, stone circle, and the Stones of Stenness - but I have missed Stromness where we stopped for lunch. Anne, Chris and I walked through the town, taking care to avoid cars which, unexpectedly, come along what are paved streets that you expect to be for pedestrians only - the coach driver did warn us! Kirkwall was the same. We saw the passageway called Khyber Pass and found a grassy sort of quayside area behind the museum (closed) with a seat overlooking the sea. On the way back to the coach we bought some Orkney cheese at a delicatessen there. The coach took us back to Kirkwall for a two hour stop, where we looked round the Cathedral after seeing an interesting video of the life of St Magnus at the St Magnus Centre next door.

We returned to the coach, now in the bus station, for our rucksacks, and the driver kindly drove us the short distance to the campsite. At first Chris had not been keen on the campsite, but when he saw it with its high wall for shelter from the strongish wind, the flower beds and bushes for windbreaks, the quietness and no crowds he changed his mind. We pitched there, made a drink of tea, had a quick bite to eat - gingerbread for me - then headed off for the Queens Hotel, recommended by the coach driver, but it had only a few tables, all reserved. The Kirkwall Hotel seemed quite expensive but had a few less expensive choices, then the Albert Hotel seemed very reasonable with Orkney salmon on the menu. We chose this quiet and pleasant eating place and I actually had a three course meal - Cream of Broccoli soup, Orkney salmon with vegetables, salad, lemon and chips, then strawberry and vanilla Orkney icecream. We all enjoyed our meal then returned to the campsite. Chris and I had been to the Leisure Centre next door/round the corner earlier to pay but found nobody there, the door locked, before 7pm. The light rain, falling when we were walking to the hotel, had now stopped. Altogether it has been a very interesting day and finished with an excellent meal to celebrate finishing LEJOG, and good friends to share it.

Sunday 16th May 2004
- John O'Groats to Duncansby Head:

I'll start at the end of the day: Here on Duncansby Head at 10.40pm I can see to write without a headtorch and it is warm enough with the tent open. The lighthouse, next to me, started flashing about 9.55pm and every eight seconds flashes into the tent. The sea is calm and silver; the sky has low grey streaks of cloud over the Orkneys with bands of pink and peach. I nipped out in my socks earlier to get a photo of the red sun below the cloud before it vanished, with the tent in the foreground. The tent is on the level cliff top near the lighthouse, about 60 yards away...

This morning we all slept late (after yesterday's early awakening!) Before we settled down for the night two cats on the high wall had been caterwauling (of course, what else would cats do on a wall?) and we found that barking at them made them move! Anyway, it was ten to eight when I looked at the time, then I quickly dressed and went for a wash then back for breakfast - Oat Bran cereal and one of those lovely brown Dunnet eggs (the hen breed began with M...) and half a brown roll. There was plenty of time before I had to leave for the 11.15am service at the Cathedral, so I washed my windshirt. A lady from Leek was pegging her washing on the revolving line so we had a chat with her. I did some packing, discussed plans with Anne and Chris, the left just before 11 o'clock, probably five to eleven.

I had time to walk round to the sunny side of the Cathedral and take a photo, although I couldn't avoid having two cars in the picture, but there was a lovely blue sky. I went in with others. It was a lovely service with an excellent choir, who sang an introit and anthem, and we had well known hymns. I really enjoyed it. Over coffee and biscuits afterwards I spoke to people from Ilkley and Bristol. The coffee was at the back of the Cathedral, poured from large flasks. Someone local said I should write something for the local paper about finishing LEJOG then celebrating on Orkney... I have still to do that. Then at 12.55 I went back to the campsite.

Chris and Anne were planning to get a bus to Stromness, the ferry to Hoy and stay a night there, which sounded very attractive, and looked attractive on the map, but they had already been to Duncansby Head and I was really wanting to go to Duncansby Head, the most north-easterly part of mainland Britain, to "complete" the walk. We agreed to meet up on Monday evening at John

O'Groats campsite. We had our lunch at the campsite then we packed. I thought I'd go up Wideford Hill, until I saw that it was about six miles of road walking in all so I went through Kirkwall to East Road and out along the track past Seatter farm to Hollands, but the sandy bay appeared not to be accessible. A friendly collie had joined me at the farm and walked with, or ahead of, me all the way, then back again to the farm. I'd stopped for a banana beside the track then I went on into Kirkwall and sat outside the Cathedral with other people waiting for the coach. It was a blue Orkney bus this time and a different driver. On the ferry I sat up on the deck in the sun - lovely - and we saw seals. The sun shone on the cliffs of South Ronaldsay and later on those of Duncansby so I took a photo of each.

After leaving the ferry a leisurely two-mile walk brought me to the lighthouse and the cliff top with soft, comfortable grass and sedge. I'd carried enough water from Orkney for the night. There was no wind. It is now 11pm, still light, still calm and peaceful. This feels right; it feels like where I should be; it feels like the real end of the walk on this northeast corner of the mainland. All is well.

Monday 17th May
- Duncansby Head southward to Freswick Bay and back to John O'Groats:

At 7 o'clock this morning the sky in the east was bright between the clouds but soon the cloud cover increased, as did the wind from the west; a few drops of rain spattered on the west side of the tent. I felt very contented here and took my time packing. It must have been 9.35 when I left, carrying a light pack now that most of the fuel and food are used. In no time I was at the trig point - is this the official end of my walk? I touched it and walked on.

This was a lovely cliff top walk with birds and flowers. The birds were mostly kittiwakes, fulmars and a few guillemots, and the flowers - masses of them! In order of the most numerous first there were: thrift, primroses, vernal squill, red campion, early purple and white orchids, white campions, and lousewort. The heather is greening and already on the crowberry there are tiny berries an eighth inch in diameter turning a dull red.

Today is a day to walk more slowly and savour the sights and sounds, the flowers, the birds, the cliffs, stacks and sea, to recall the delights of past weeks and miles. This still feels right for me to be here, the place where I should be, following on round the coast from John O'Groats and it is so spectacular that I am sure I shall return along the cliffs this afternoon, rather than by lane and road, especially as, according to the forecast, there is a hope of some sunshine this afternoon. I have stopped to write this at my 11.30am break sitting on the heather; otherwise I probably should not have noticed the tiny berries on the crowberry. Onward now to enjoy!

A track led from an old quarry to a farm, then a lane continued past houses and crofts and a harbour sign until a path on the left led down to the beach at Freswick Bay. Here dunlin and oystercatchers searched the tideline and seaweed. I had lunch in a sheltered gateway just above the beach then I went down to the sea to take a photo at my most southerly point from Duncansby, now with sun and blue sky. Perhaps here was the real end of the walk? Back now past the farms and cottages then I cut in past the quarry to the cliffs with their rich display of flowers. There were some that I had not recorded this morning: deep purple violets, white scurvy grass, plantains, one single bird's foot trefoil, several pink and white flowers of chickweed wintergreen and some early tormentil, and more and more thrift in varying shades of pink with the light blue vernal squill scattered in the grass between the banks of thrift. In the damper heathery areas there was the odd white tuft of hare's tail cotton grass, and I saw the leaves of what I now know is Scots lovage. Near Wife Geo there was dwarf willow. After following the spring north I had a wonderful display of spring flowers to make the last day memorable.

Although the sunny spells increased this afternoon the wind strength also increased from the west, making forward progress a bit difficult, and northward progress along cliff edges a bit cautious. I wonder what the ferry will be like for Anne and Chris returning to JOG? - a bit rough, they told me later - sometimes the propeller came out of the water and the engine stopped. The wind continued, now blowing dark clouds into the blue sky as I pressed on northward. Soon Duncansby Stacks were ahead with an abundance of thrift in the foreground - the ideal photo, which, sadly, left only one more exposure on the film, which I took from the north side of the Stacks, again with some thrift on the cliff top in the foreground. The path rose on soft grass towards the lighthouse; I reached the road and walked the two miles to John O'Groats while curlew, lapwing and sheep announced their presence on all sides.

I went to the John O'Groats shop for the last time, for eggs, an apple and some more of the delicious Walkers Gingerbread cake, then down to the campsite and returned to our sheltered corner under the "rhubarb bank" by the sea. My last meal of the walk, apart from breakfast, was soon under way, with some nettles from the Duncansby lane, but before I'd got round to pudding I heard the ferry, looked out and reckoned that, in a few minutes, both it and I would reach the quay so, sandals on, I went to meet Anne and Chris and hear their news as we walked back together. Quite a wind now - I changed zips then had my fruit salad and yoghurt, then went to wash up and wash self, underwear and socks before we all went down to the John O'Groats Hotel for the last time.

Now, on Tuesday morning, breakfast is over; our bus from John O'Groats to Thurso leaves mid-morning for the train to Inverness. I'm sitting in the tent watching the waves breaking and hearing the ferry, or another boat, round the corner. Grey Orkney Islands lie across a grey sea. This was the holiday of a lifetime, living my dream, with new experiences every day. "Follow the Spring North!" "Live your dream!" "It is still there - keep smiling!" Thanks be to God.

LAND'S END TO JOHN O'GROATS

WILD FLOWERS MARCH TO MAY

Dandelion	Taraxacum officinale
Dog's Mercury	Mercurialis perennis
Buttercup	Ranunculas acris
Wood anemone	Anemone nemorosa
Lesser celandine	Ranunculus ficaria
Marsh Marigold	Caltha palustris
Cuckoo flower, Lady's Smock	Cardamine pratensis
Garlic mustard	Alliaria petiolata
Common scurvy grass	Cochlearia officinalis
Heath Milkwort	Polygola serpyllifolia
Sweet violet	Viola odorata
Common violet	Viola riviniana
Bog violet	Viola palustris
Sea campion	Silene maritime
Bladder campion	Silene vulgaris
Red campion	Silene dioica
Greater Stitchwort	Stellaria holostea
....Montia perfoliata	(like chickweed with large leaf)
Herb Robert	Geranium robertianum
Gorse	Ulex europaeus
Red clover	Trifolium pratense
Bird's foot trefoil	Lotus corniculatus
Tormentil	Potentilla erecta
Water avens	Geum rivale
Golden saxifrage	Chrysosplenium oppositifolium
Daisy	Bellis perennis
Coltsfoot	Tussilago farfara
Butterbur	Pelesites hybridus
Bilberry	Vaccinium myrtillus
Crowberry	Empitrum nigrum
Thrift	Aremria maritime
Primrose	Primula vulgaris
Chickweed wintergreen	Trientalis europaea
Cowslip	Primula veris
Periwinkle	Vinca Minor

Common forget-me-not	Mysotis arvensis
Germander speedwell	Veronica chamaedrys
Lousewort	Pedicularis sylvatica
Early purple orchid	Orchis mascula
Triangular stalked garlic}	Allium triquetrum
Three cornered leek	
Ramsons	Allium Ursinum
Vernal Squill	Scilla verna
Bluebell	Endymion non-scriptus
Field wood-rush	Luzula campestris
Great wood-rush	Luzula sylvatica
Wood sorrel	Oxalis acetosetta

The plan was to "Follow the Spring North" so that it would be spring in Cornwall in March and Spring in Scotland in May. This would also mean finishing before the midge season in Scotland, and before the weather became too hot for walking. The spring flowers all the way up the country were a great attraction.

LAND'S END TO JOHN O'GROATS

BIRDS
- MARCH TO MAY

Curlew	Puffin
Golden Plover	Guillemot
Snipe	Fulmar
Lapwing	Kittiwake
Common Sandpiper	Cormorant
Dipper	Herring Gull
Skylark	Gt. Black backed Gull
Meadow Pipit	Canada Goose
Oystercatcher	Mallard
Dunlin	Eider Duck
Kestrel	Moorhen
Hen Harrier	Great Crested Grebe
Peregrine	Redshank
Ring Ouzel	Wood pigeon
Wheatear	Green Woodpecker
Wren	Pheasant
Blackbird	Crow
Yellowhammer	Rook
Song thrush	Cuckoo
Heron	Sparrow
Stonechat	Chiffchaff
Long Tailed Tit	Greenfinch
Great Tit	Robin
Blue tit	Chaffinch
Grey wagtail	Buzzard
Pied Wagtail	Grouse
Mute Swan	Golden Eye

Only one each seen of: Stonechat (North Coast near Reay), Cuckoo, Ring Ouzel, Peregrine and Puffin (Dunnet Head) - all in Scotland.

THE STRESS FRACTURE

Three questions I was asked at the hospital: "Did you fall?" " No." " Does anyone in the family suffer from osteoporosis?" " No." " Do you have a good diet?" " Yes."

So why did it happen? It seems most probable that it was due to the jarring on hard roads when I had many miles of road walking particularly on the Dulverton to Taunton day, and the next couple of days were each 20 miles; from Dulverton to Taunton had been 7 miles on footpaths and 13 miles on roads, at a fair pace to try to reach Taunton before dark. These miles were also with a heavy pack and, looking back, I remember feeling the jarring to my left heel during the few miles before Taunton. If those footpaths in that area had been walkable it would have made a difference having a softer surface to walk on. In any case I don't like walking on roads with traffic rushing past so prefer footpaths and bridleways.

Of course, I did not know that the pain was caused by a fracture so I carried on walking, or hobbling, and it even seemed to feel better by the following Thursday morning, then worse again going down the hill to Painswick. Could this have been because the crack only went part way through the bone before this, then the loose stones before the footbridge gave it a jerk and it was worse after this, possibly because the crack now went right through? I don't know. Anyway, it healed quickly.

Before I started again in March 2004 someone said, "So you're going to have another crack at it? Oh, that's not the right word, is it?" I was already planning to avoid "another crack" and the previous June, while still on crutches, I had bought a pair of Sorbothane heel pads to act as shock absorbers, so that any unavoidable road walking would not cause the same jarring to the bones. I had thought about diet, and realised that, while backpacking, I only carried enough milk powder for ½ pint milk per day, instead of the recommended 1 pint. Therefore, I would buy fresh milk when I could, and take calcium tablets on the days when I couldn't buy a pint of milk. I have also read that calcium can be lost in perspiration. I had cheese in a roll for lunch most days. When I had my final check up at the hospital in March (after walking from Cheltenham to Macclesfield) the doctor said, "Is there anything you want to ask me?" All I could think of was, "Do you think that Sorbothane heel pads in my boots are a good idea?" "Yes, I do," was his reply.

One thing I discovered about the Sorbothane heel pads was that they threw my weight slightly forward on to my toes, which is probably why some people had told me that they had tried the heel pads and not got on with them. (They are about ¼ inch thick). I was actually sore under my big toes for a few days, not the first two or three days from Witcombe but certainly the day I walked into Lichfield, and sometimes muscles in my feet ached a bit from being in a slightly different position. I think the soreness and aching lasted about five days; I don't remember any problems on the day I walked into Macclesfield, in spite of some of this being on roads due to the canal towpath being closed, and certainly my feet must have got used to the new walking position because I had no problems after that. There was even quite a bit of road walking along the north coast of Scotland so the Sorbothane heel pads obviously did their job on the 850 miles from Cheltenham!

Did I get back 95% of my walking ability, as I was told on 1st April 2003? I had absolutely no problems with my hip and would not know that it was any different from the other one. I wondered if I'd have less movement when lifting it over a stile, but no problem at all. The only time it aches is when I sit for a long time, as for a long drive. I have a small scar, only ¾ inch long, but my walking seems completely unaffected. I would say that I have got back 105% of my walking ability!

FOOD FOR THE WALK

This was what took most organising and preparing. For a walk of that length, that was expected to last three months, food parcels had to be sent in advance, or given to friends who were meeting me along the route. The foods bought as I went along included eggs, fresh milk, fresh fruit, tomatoes, occasionally a carrot, rolls or bread and cheese, yoghurt, chocolate, cakes. The foods I carried had to be lightweight so food parcels contained dehydrated foods and a few packets, e.g. Cheese Sauce mix, instant mashed potato and Cadbury's Chocolate Dessert. The food needed to be nutritious and something that I could look forward to at the end of the day.

Food dehydrated in 2002/3 went in the parcels that were posted off in early 2003. I have a dehydrator, a Harvest Maid Snack-maker, which I have had for seven years. These are now sold under the name of Ezidri. Using this I could dehydrate cooked, finely chopped or minced beef, lamb, pork, chicken, turkey, liver, chopped flaked steamed fish (coley and haddock), cooked lentils and other pulses, a variety of vegetables, so that I could have two or three different vegetables with each meal, a variety of fruits for fruit salad, fruit crumble, fruit and custard or fruit with semolina. Dehydrated bananas made a good snack. With the meat, fish or lentils I had either instant mash, pasta or "instant" rice. This is cooked long-grain rice, dehydrated, which then returns to its original weight and only needs to have boiling water poured on then stand for five minutes while other food is cooking. Couscous was also used.

Packets of cheese sauce were used with macaroni and dehydrated cauliflower and onion or leek, but other sauces were made by putting in a bag some cornflour, sometimes with milk powder, pepper, herbs or pure ground garlic or dehydrated mushrooms. Turkey in garlic sauce was particularly good, and dehydrated rosemary went well with the lamb and parsley with the fish. These sauces made good thickeners for the cooking liquid. One of the first jobs after fetching water each evening was to put the dehydrated food to soak in a pan, then it only needed a few minutes simmering. Sometimes I would use a complete dehydrated meal, but these did not keep their flavour as well as the separate vegetables, which had only been blanched, not cooked, before dehydrating. I looked forward to my meals and, after picking up a food parcel, often chose the heaviest first to save weight in the pack....or sometimes I would choose the one that would cook in the shortest time, if very hungry or arrived a bit late.

Fresh fruit, of course, is heavy, so only one or two would be carried at a time, depending on where I expected my next supply to be. The only fresh vegetable I bought was a carrot now and then, because sprouts were no longer around and what else can you buy in an individual size? You don't want the weight and bulk of a whole cabbage or cauliflower and, while a tomato could be added to the cheese roll for lunch, a lettuce would not keep until I had finished it so there might be a shortage of greens. This was solved by using wild greens: leaves of dandelion, chickweed and garlic mustard, the latter in particular, went well with cheese or sardines. The only tins I used were sardines, sild and a tin of chopped ham and pork. I have, in the past, used tins of herring roes and cod roes but I didn't come across these during LEJOG. Many village shops would be limited in the variety they could stock, but even so, I managed to get most things that I needed in these friendly village shops. Cereals were muesli, porridge, and Puffed Wheat, which is very light in weight.

Fuel for the Trangia was meths; I found that, with care, half a litre would last for a week, especially when using a campsite so that I did not need to heat water for washing. It was not possible to post the meths in food parcels so it went in those parcels given to friends and I was able to carry a litre from Land's End and from Edinburgh, and to buy some at Inverness so the fuel worked out all right.

VILLAGES/TOWNS WITH SHOPS

(*** denotes a particularly friendly, helpful shop*)
Cornwall:
St Ives, Hayle, Newquay, Constantine Bay, Padstow, St Mabyn**
Launceston,
Devon:
Northlew, Hatherleigh.
Somerset:
Dulverton, Taunton, Glastonbury, Wells, Bath, Saltford.
Gloucestershire: Old Sodbury, Kings Stanley**, Painswick, Winchcombe, Chipping Campden
Worcestershire, Warwickshire and West Midlands:
Mickleton, Bidford-on-Avon, Alcester, Henley-on-Arden, Meriden
Staffordshire:
Lichfield, Abbott's Bromley**, Uttoxeter, Rocester
Cheshire:
Macclesfield, Marple, Compstall
Yorkshire:
Hebden Bridge, Gargrave, Horton-in-Ribblesdale**,Hawes.
Middleton-in-Teesdale to Byrness:
Middleton-in-Teesdale, Garrigill, Alston, Haltwhistle, Bellingham,
Scotland South of Edinburgh:
Town Yetholm, Greenlaw, Gifford, Haddington, Aberlady, Prestonpans, Musselburgh.
Scotland, Edinburgh and northward: Edinburgh, South Queensferry, Inverkeithing, Aberdour, Kirkcaldy, Thornton, Glenrothes, Bridge of Earn, Methven, Aberfeldy**, Pitlochry, Blair Atholl, Kincraig, Farr/Inverarnie** (corner of B861, Inverness, North Kessock, Munlochy, Evanton, Ardgay**, Bonar Bridge, Lairg, Melvich/ Porthskerra, Reay, Thurso, John O'Groats**

EQUIPMENT AND CLOTHING USED
FOR THE WALK

Item	Make	Weight
Tent	Saunders Spacepacker *(I like choice of 4 zips on flysheet for sunrise/sunset or change of wind direction and plenty of storage space).*	4lbs
Sleeping Bag	Mountain Equipment Dewline	1lb 7ozs
Sleeping bag cover	Home-made from Pertex	5ozs
Stove	Trangia 27K *(Used without frying pan but with kettle- reliable, trouble-free.)*	1lb 12ozs
Mug	Titanium	2ozs
Knife, fork, spoon	? Army & Navy stores	2ozs
Insulation mat	Z Rest *(half of it used)*	8ozs
Sit mat	*(Goes under feet at night).*	
	Free years ago!	¾ oz
Rucksack	GoLite Gust	1lb 6ozs
Towel	Life Venture Trek *(without its zip-up case)*	5 ozs
Wash kit	Caledonian Sleeper + extras	6ozs

First aid kit - items most likely to be needed - 6ozs including tea tree oil. Poly bag containing: candle, matches, 2 clothes pegs, spare toilet paper, piece cut from nylon tights to strain bits of moss etc out of water. 2¼ ozs

Toilet trowel	Grassroots	1½ ozs
Head torch	Princeton Aurora Tech	2½ ozs
Waterbag	Ortlieb	2½ ozs
Waterbottles (2)	Platypus 1 litre	1oz each
Map case	Ortlieb+ compass & pen	3½ ozs
Sponge/scourer, mini scourer,		
Wipe ups (tea towels)		1oz
Tupperware bowl	to wash in/carry eggs in	4ozs
Compact camera	Cannon Sureshot	9ozs
Waterproof case	Aquapac	3ozs
Mobile phone	Aquapac case	5½ ozs

Waist bag	Lowe Alpine	6ozs
Wallet	Lowe Alpine + average contents	6ozs
Small binoculars + case	Praktica Sport Compact *(carried on belt of waist bag).*	8½ ozs

   The only items bought specially for the walk were the Aquapac waterproof camera case and mobile phone case; the rest of the equipment was well tried and tested.

Total weight of the above items: 13lbs 13ozs.

CLOTHING.

Trousers	Craghoppers Kiwi (zip off to shorts)
T-shirts	one Lowe Alpine and
	one North Cape Coolmax
Warm top	North Cape Rhovyl turtleneck
Windshirt	Buffalo *(green, no hood,*
	excellent lightweight garment)
Waterproofs	Gore-Tex, Rock & Run.
	(old, re-proofed)
Overtrousers:	Gelert, (cheap lightweight)
Woolly hat	Homemade, headover type, pure wool
	- keeps ears, head and neck warm.
Gloves 1)	Homemade nylon showerproof
	with fibre pile inner
Gloves 2)	Thin liner gloves
Spare trousers/nightwear	Ron Hill Tracksters
Spare top/nightwear	Damart long sleeved top, old,
	very lightweight
Underwear, 2 sets	Lowe Alpine, very quick drying
Socks, thick, 2 pairs	Smartwool - kindly donated by
	Smartwool - and Bridgedale Merino
Socks, thin liner	2 pairs Coolmax (quick drying)
Boots	Scarpa Lady Ranger (later with
	added Sorbothane Heel pads)
Boot proofing	Nikwax Aqueous wax - kindly
	donated by Nikwax

Clothing was washed in environmentally friendly coconut oil based liquid from Natural Collection, which was carried in a small shampoo bottle in the wash kit.

People Mentioned In Diary

- AND THANKS TO THEM ALL.

Since the Diary was originally written to record the memories for me to read myself in later years I did not need to explain in the text who the people were, but for other readers I'll add a note: *Family*: Maurice and Julie - my older son and his, then, girlfriend; Trevor and Nicky - my younger son and his wife. Paula - daughter (mentioned on Pennine Way). My father - the frequent phone calls were because at age 91-92, living alone, he wanted to know how I was getting on. Malcolm and Margaret - my brother and sister-in-law, with whom I spent a night. I also spent a night with my cousin, Jean, and her husband, Arthur, and my Auntie Alice and two other cousins, Wendy & Derek, came to see us that evening.

Backpackers Club members: Tony Wilson whom I contacted to update his website of my route, Geoff & Wendy Trevarthen, Lynette Corr, Ros & Stuart Boase, Dave & Liz Lee, Sandra & Brian Haigh, Will Bankes, Val Self and Rose McKenzie all of whom kindly took food parcels. Julia Griffiths, Dave Britton, and others on Wookey weekend. Jim & Maggie Beed. Anne Ling & Chris Barnes who walked the first and last few days with me. Cameron McNeish for his encouraging e-mail message. Allan Carter and Geoff Boyling who lent me books. Pat & Steve Rich and Lawrence & Lesley Dark, who put me up for a night and fed me. Bryan Crick & Ron Johnson (walked LEJOG in 2003). *Friends at St Mary's Church, Sandbach*: Some are mentioned for their much appreciated help after my injury: Anita, Bob & June, Stella, Katie and many others.

Great thanks to all of you.

USEFUL ADDRESSES

BACKPACKERS CLUB, Membership Secretary: Roy
Clayton, 24 Chequer's Place, Cholsey,
Wallingford, Oxfordshire OX10 9PF
 E-mail: Roy@clayton-family.freeserve.co.uk

YHA, Trevelyan House, Dimple Road, Matlock,
Derbyshire DE4 3YH www.yha.org.uk
Tel: 0870 770 8868

LAND'S END TO JOHN O'GROATS CLUB. Cilla
George, Land's End to John O'Groats Club, Custom
House, Sennen, Penzance, Cornwall TR19 7AA
 Tel: 0870 4580044 Ext 322 or 01736 810287
 E-mail: cillageorge@aol.com

The Independent Hostel Guide. The Backpackers Press, 2
Rockview Cottages, Matlock Bath, Derbyshire DE4 3PG.
Tel/fax: 01629 580427 E-mail DaveDalley@aol.com

John O'Groats Ferries (to Orkney) tel:01955 611353
www.jogferry.co.uk

ISBN 141202635-0